"Chad has an incredible outlook on life, whether it be sports, music, fashion, or more important, his walk in Faith. I am thankful God placed Chad in my life to reveal who he is and how much he loves us. I pray this book will provide an abundance of insight and increase your walk with God as well."

—GOLDEN TATE, NFL WIDE RECEIVER

"I'm very proud to call Chad and Julia not only friends but a big part of my LA family, and I know through this book they will touch people's lives like they've touched mine."

—HAILEY BALDWIN, FASHION MODEL

"Chad Veach is a contagious person. Whenever I am around him it's good vibes, fun, and full of laughs. He inspires me to be the best person I can be and I hope this book does the same for you!"

—RICKIE FOWLER, PGA GOLFER, 2015 PLAYERS CHAMPION

"Authentic and Inspiring. *Unreasonable Hope* will take you on a journey that will leave you hopeful and encouraged. The story of Chad and Julia's faith through the toughest of days will challenge you and build your confidence in Jesus. This book reminds us that God paints on a canvas bigger than we can see or imagine. Hope has a name, and His name is Jesus!"

—LOUIE GIGLIO, PASTOR, PASSION CITY CHURCH AND PASSION CONFERENCES

"With this story, Chad Veach will continue to touch, motivate, and transform lives around the world."

—TYSON CHANDLER, NBA ALL-STAR, NBA CHAMPION, AND OLYMPIC GOLD MEDALIST

"It's one thing to be positive, hopeful, and passionate about life when LIFE IS GOOD. The true test of joy, however, is how we function when life is inexplicably complicated and painful. I want to learn and glean from people who continually pass this test of 'joy in all circumstances.' Chad and Julia? I simply don't know people who can maintain a joyful spirit through all seasons of life like them. This book will be an anchor of hope for many, as we all navigate the uncharted waters of this life."

—CARL LENTZ, LEAD PASTOR, HILLSONG CHURCH, NEW YORK CITY

"My friend Chad Veach delivers the kind of message that jumps off the pages and directly into your heart. I'm not sure I've read a book so profound yet so accessible. In these days we live in, Hope is essential and Chad helps us procure it in a significant and beautiful way!"

—ISRAEL HOUGHTON, RECORDING ARTIST AND WORSHIP
LEADER AT LAKEWOOD CHURCH, HOUSTON, TEXAS

"It is with great admiration that I have watched this young family live out their faith testimony on a public platform—courageously choosing to rise above their own circumstance with a love, faith, and hopeful patience that draws people to wonder why. Chad's obvious love for others and contagiously joyful spirit compels you to discover more of the God he is so passionate about—and his personal walk through trial and triumph will leave you with no doubt that our God can indeed bring about great purpose in seasons of great pain. We will never stop #PrayingForGeorgia."

—BRIAN HOUSTON, FOUNDER AND GLOBAL
SENIOR PASTOR OF HILLSONG CHURCH

"Chad's greatest sermon is that 'Hope has a name: Jesus.' He taught me this with his life. Not from the stage. The stage of life is the greatest platform and Chad and Julia encourage us every day that we serve a God greater than any circumstance. I'm thankful for his friendship and example of God's love."

—JERRY LORENZO, FASHION DESIGNER

"It's said about a very select group of people that when they walk into a room, it lights up. Ignoring any excuse to do the contrary, Chad brings a light that is infectious and engulfing of any heaviness. I got a G tattooed on my forearm as a representation of the belief and the hope I stand in with Chad, Julia, and Georgia. It's a representation of the hope that is available in every situation. It's a representation of defeated darkness and ever-present light no matter the size of the shadowed diagnosis. Our hope is alive and living. I'm thankful for Chad and Julia and the tangible proof they show in their amazing Georgia."

—RYAN GOOD, STYLIST FOR JUSTIN BIEBER, ACTOR,
AND PRODUCER OF THE TV SHOW PUNK'D

"With raw honesty and infectious faith, Chad Veach reveals his encounter with God's promises when his infant daughter was diagnosed with a rare brain disorder. The result is a book you will read, reread, and give to others who struggle with pain. *Unreasonable Hope* speaks to the doubt, fear, and uncertainty we all experience when life goes off the rails—and transforms them into the peace, joy, and hope that comes from trusting God."

—CHRIS HODGES, SENIOR PASTOR, CHURCH OF THE HIGHLANDS; AUTHOR OF *FRESH AIR* AND *FOUR CUPS*

"[Georgia's] influence has been profound and far reaching already and with the telling of her story through this book, it is set to spread even further, reminding us of this powerful force that the Bible tells us will remain along with faith and love: (unreasonable) hope."

—BROOKE FRASER, MUSIC ARTIST

"*Unreasonable Hope* holds the keys to one of the great questions of life: How can we find purpose in our pain? This book will inspire anyone who is struggling to feel love and grace during life's worst moments."

—JENTEZEN FRANKLIN, SENIOR PASTOR, FREE CHAPEL; *NEW YORK TIMES* BESTSELLING AUTHOR

UNREASONABLE
HOPE

UNREASONABLE HOPE

Finding Faith in the God Who
Brings Purpose to Your Pain

CHAD VEACH

NELSON
BOOKS

An Imprint of Thomas Nelson

Published in Nashville, Tennessee, by Nelson Books, an imprint of Thomas Nelson. Nelson Books and Thomas Nelson are registered trademarks of HarperCollins Christian Publishing, Inc.

Published in association with the literary agency of The FEDD Agency, Inc., P.O. Box 341973, Austin, Texas, 78734.

Thomas Nelson titles may be purchased in bulk for educational, business, fundraising, or sales promotional use. For information, please e-mail SpecialMarkets@ ThomasNelson.com.

Library of Congress Cataloging-in-Publication Data

Names: Veach, Chad, 1979-
Title: Unreasonable hope: finding faith in the God who brings purpose to your pain / Chad Veach.
Description: Nashville: Thomas Nelson, 2016. | Includes bibliographical references.
Identifiers: LCCN 2015032142 | ISBN 9780718038342
Subjects: LCSH: Suffering--Religious aspects--Christianity.
Classification: LCC BV4909 .V43 2016 | DDC 248.8/6--dc23 LC record available at http://lccn.loc.gov/2015032142

Printed in the United States of America

16 17 18 19 20 RRD 5 4 3 2

To my Julia.
Your love, patience, and sacrifice through all of this is incomparable.
You are my hero and I love you with all my heart.

CONTENTS

CONTENTS

FOREWORD

I AM CONVINCED THAT THE HOPE THAT GROWS IN TIMES OF trial is the most beautiful hope.

Georgia taught me that.

Georgia is Chad and Julia's young daughter. She has a rare brain disorder called lissencephaly. I remember when Chad and Julia, who have been friends of mine for years, first heard the diagnosis. I was out of town with my family. We already knew there was some kind of complication, but we didn't know how serious it was or what it would mean for the Veach family.

Chad called to give me the doctor's report, and I'll never forget the strain in his voice. The knot in his throat. The tears I could hear even over the phone. But more than that, I will never forget Chad's faithfulness and unwavering belief that God is good—all the time, in every way, no matter what. From the very beginning, Chad chose hope and trust when self-pity and bitterness would have been the easier road.

We cried together that day. But we also understood that GiGi is a gift from God. A miracle. Perfectly planned and formed by a God who knows no limitations.

The doctors said GiGi would never be responsive. They said she would never turn her head, open her eyes, or smile at the parents who loved her unconditionally. We were told to stop believing and to stop hoping.

But that's not Chad. He can't stop hoping. Faith and joy and hope are hardwired into him. Anyone who has spent thirty seconds with him could tell you that.

Chad's personality is fun, electric, and ridiculously loud. In the best possible way, of course. But it is his faith that leaves the greatest impact. His unswerving hope literally changes you. I know, because it has changed me. I've watched and learned as Chad and Julia have faced fear without faltering. Their capacity to hope despite impossible odds is as astounding as it is inspiring. They never stop believing, never stop praying, never stop hoping.

What Chad and Julia have gone through is unique, of course. But we can all relate to struggles. Maybe for you and me, the struggles we face are different: broken relationships, tragedies, failures. The point isn't to compare pain, but to learn how to hope in the face of pain.

And that is what Chad and Julia do better than anyone I know.

The other day Chad sent me a video of GiGi. I couldn't keep the tears from my eyes as I watched her clearly, unmistakably responding to what her dad was saying. She made eye contact. She smiled. She radiated joy.

These are the miracles that follow hope. To see GiGi is to realize how precious life is—and how essential hope is.

Unreasonable Hope reminds us to look to Jesus and respond to his love and grace in life's worst moments. Chad's stories, passion, and wisdom will inspire you—even in the most unreasonable circumstances—to hope again.

Judah Smith

Part 1

THE STRUGGLE

It Happened One Night

What does every parent want more than anything? More than success for their child or a long list of accolades, what thought most consumes a mom and a dad? True, almost all parents have some crazy vision of their kids as the next Michael Jordan or Steve Jobs. Without meaning to, we occasionally imagine our child's name in shining lights on a marquee or in a newspaper's headline. But there's another desire that's even more present. Something all parents want more than an overachieving star child. It's a desire that can haunt you at strange hours of the night, wake you from a deep sleep, and pop into your head when you least expect it.

Safety.

We want our kids to achieve great things, to "live the dream" and "have it all." But more than this, we want them to be safe from harm. From the moment we strap their little bodies into oversized car seats, we're worried. Suddenly the freeway becomes a death trap, everyone is a crazy driver, and our vehicles won't move at speeds above thirty-five miles an hour. This is all because we are responsible for the little lives strapped in the back of our cars. No one is going to mess with our babies.

My wife, Julia, and I are no exception to the rule. In fact, if the range of caution is measured on a scale from Hippy-Let-Your-Child-Be-Free Parents to Paranoid-Never-Let-Your-Child-Be-

3

More-Than-Three-Feet-Away Parents, Julia and I might be a little too close to becoming full-time residents at a mental institution.

Our paranoia was perhaps strongest when it came to our first child and most definitely evident when it came to the baby monitor. A baby monitor is a lovely device that allows you to hear your child sleeping. If your child happens to stir in the night, you will hear it and come flying to her aid. It's a beautiful miracle of technology!

It's also the most annoying thing on the planet.

We knew Julia would be going back to work only a few months after our daughter, Georgia, was born, so we wanted to train her to sleep away from us. We were determined not to have a co-sleeper and to get her used to the idea of her parents being in the room next door. We were going to be strong! Doesn't quite sound like the paranoid parents I was describing, does it?

Well, in our attempt to "be strong," we found ourselves the exact opposite. Every night, we'd lay the baby monitor between our heads with the volume set to "ear-shattering, full blast."

If Georgia cried, we wanted to hear it. We also heard if a feather dropped in the room or a mouse sneezed. Every night, we were lulled to sleep by the loudest, most irritating static. And if we were lucky, we'd pick up a frequency from some car driving down the street nearby or the neighbor's satellite television.

It was anything but peaceful. One night while this static blasted in my ear, sounding like someone crunching a thousand candy wrappers at once, I snapped. Something came over me. I realized how the Incredible Hulk must feel, and the baby monitor became the victim of my anger. That miracle of technology went flying through the room, right out the door, and into the hallway, smashing into the wall with a *crack*!

"Enough!" I yelled, returning to my sleeping position with a newfound admiration for silence.

It was only five minutes later, however, that I became filled with regret. As Julia and I settled back into sleep, our paranoia, the reason we had the monitor blasting in the first place, returned. I found myself reluctantly walking back into the hall to grab the monitor, pop the batteries back in, and return to the bed, tucking the monitor next to my head, volume at its previous ear-shattering level.

If our perfect little girl needed me, I would be ready.

During those first couple of months, this is how we viewed our Georgia. She was perfect in every way. So perfect that it seemed all of our baby monitor craziness wasn't really needed. We rarely heard her cry through the monitor's static. In fact, she rarely cried at all. At the time, we didn't realize that was *not* a good thing. But I'll get into that later.

For now, you only need to know that we soon discovered our little girl was not safe from harm. But it wasn't crazy drivers or broken baby monitors that threatened to take our daughter from us. It was something much uglier.

It was *lissencephaly.*

Don't worry. We'd never heard of it either. That is, until April 10, 2012, a little over four months after Georgia was born. Soon I will delve into this terrible day, how it affected our family, and the details of what lissencephaly means. For now, though, you just need to know that it has to do with our daughter's brain and her inability to function normally. It also comes with many terrible side effects.

One of the worst of these is the tendency toward seizures and spasms.

Infantile spasms are awful to watch. Imagine an electric shock wave traveling through the body in short bursts. The baby will have this wave and then return to consciousness for a moment before having another. The waves may appear again and again in a terrible pattern. But for the most part, they are not life threatening.

Seizures, by comparison, are much worse. A seizure can occur at any age. They are violent and ugly. While having a seizure, a person or child will shake all over uncontrollably. Her eyes will roll into the back of their heads, and the whole ordeal can drag on for minutes or come in clusters. This means that the first seizure of the day will most likely not be the last.

Months after we received Georgia's diagnosis, this is what we faced on a daily basis.

If we were paranoid before all this went down, there is no word to describe what we were next. Our days in the months following April 10 were filled with constant worry. There wasn't a baby monitor loud enough to give us peace of mind once we discovered what exactly our daughter was up against.

I always like to joke that my wife has job security. Without her, I have no idea what I'm doing. In times of crisis, my MO is to stand with wide, blank eyes and ask her, "What should we do?"

I ask this question because Julia is brilliant. She's quick to answer and problem-solve, she's smart with money, she plans every vacation and major life event, and basically, I can't live without her. I know it sounds very mushy and romantic, but it's also a practical reality. I need Julia Veach.

Even before Georgia was born, I often asked Julia, "What should we do?" Because I'm a pastor, I'm constantly traveling to speak at different churches, and I always end up leaving something in the hotel room. Among the many things accidentally abandoned at Hiltons across the globe are watches, sweaters, cologne, and two brand-new suit jackets. If it's an inanimate object, I've left it.

Usually what occurs is a sudden onset of memory when I finally get home. Yes, it seems that it's always upon arrival that I realize an item has been left behind. This is when I turn to Julia. This is where she shines. In five minutes she's called the hotel lobby and arranged the shipping, and because of her superpowers, the lost item arrives on our doorstep the following morning.

Because I am utterly helpless when losing even something trivial like my cologne, I had no idea what to do when Georgia started having infantile spasms and, soon after, full-on seizures. I stood there like a deer in the headlights as Julia talked to the doctors on the phone.

What do we do now? The question ran through my mind. *This isn't supposed to happen. This can't be happening. How do we stop the seizures? How do we take away this disorder? How do we prevent all this?*

The reality was that the doctors had put a life sentence on my daughter. They told us that children with the disorder have a life expectancy of about ten years. Many die much earlier than that. It seemed that no matter what we tried, the clock was ticking.

This meant every time a seizure occurred, we were holding our breaths as if plunging into the ocean. *Could this be the moment? Is this the day you're going to take her from us, God?*

Our first-time-parent guilt was now joined by new-caretaker guilt. We found ourselves constantly haunted by the question of whether we were caring for Georgia in the right way, whether there was something we should be trying or doing differently.

And this haunting feeling only worsened when Georgia's seizures began at the end of May 2012.

The summer came next, as summers tend to do after spring. Seasons are predictable that way. With it came City Blast, a giant event put on by our church to celebrate the Fourth of July with the community. As I was on staff at the church, Julia and I had large roles to play in this event. There was a basketball tournament run by yours truly (I'm kind of a wannabe LeBron). There was also a large 10K race in which we had both committed to participate. The event was huge in the city. People would come from all over for a perfect summer day.

Georgia, however, didn't know about this, and she, along with her disorder, had other plans for the week.

On July 2, Julia and I lay sleeping in our bed. Well, I was sleeping. I had somehow drifted off into a hard snooze even with the baby monitor blaring. I was out cold. Julia, on the other hand, lay awake, listening intently as she always tended to do.

Her hands grasped the comforter as her ears worked at 115 percent. She waited to hear a change in Georgia's breath that signified something was wrong. When a seizure hit, neither screaming nor crying blasted through the monitor. No, when a seizure hit, all that could be heard amid the static was a slight change in the pace of our girl's breath—a small inconsistency. We would hear a pause, followed by short, deep bursts of breath.

I'm sure it wouldn't be very noticeable to most ears. It definitely wouldn't wake you up from a deep sleep. Often I would sleep through it. Lauren, a friend who lived with us and helped out with Georgia, would sleep through it as well. But sleep wasn't in the cards for Julia that night. She lay awake with a deep sense of worry and anxiety.

Is Georgia okay? she wondered.

Is she breathing right now? Will tonight be the night? If tonight is the night, will it have been my fault? Will I have questions? Will I blame myself? How will Chad take it?

When I look back on our story and our journey so far with Georgia's condition, this night, July 2, 2012, stands out very clearly in my mind as a moment when something beyond just Julia and me, someone bigger than our little family's struggles, intervened.

"Chad!"

I woke to my name and someone shaking my body. I started to drift back to sleep, the darkness closing in, when . . .

"Chad!" Julia yelled again. She was adamant that we needed to talk.

Instantly, my mind went to Georgia. "What? Do we need to

go to the doctor? Is Georgia okay?" I began to wake up. I searched around the room for my glasses so I could see what was going on.

"No. It's not that. I need to have a conversation with you," Julia said. Her tone was serious.

A conversation? I thought. Most conversations can usually wait for the morning, after coffee. This better be good.

But what came next was unexpected.

"I need to know that if Georgia were to die tonight, you wouldn't blame me."

"What? Julia, I—"

"I need to know," she interrupted. "I need to know that if God were to take her while we slept, if she were to have a seizure or choke or stop breathing, that you would feel that we both tried everything we could to help her. I need to know that you wouldn't blame me and that you wouldn't blame yourself."

It completely threw me off. First of all, why would Julia ever assume that I would blame her for something as terrible as that? In that moment, I realized how much guilt she was carrying over the whole situation. And then I thought about myself.

How often had I experienced the same sort of worry? How often had I, too, lay awake wondering if Georgia would live to see the next morning, worrying if there was something I could've done differently? We were both carrying the guilt for something we didn't do.

"Of course I wouldn't," I answered sincerely.

And it was the truth. Somehow, in that moment, God had stirred this question inside of Julia, which had caused her to wake me up. He wanted us both to give Georgia's situation to him. He wanted us to admit what was out of our control, to give the entire thing to him and let him take over.

We weren't going to blame ourselves anymore.

Julia and I both slept much more peacefully that night. She's told me before that it was the first solid night of sleep she'd had since Georgia was born. The whole situation was rather strange. Why had God chosen to wake us up at this moment? Why had we suddenly realized that we needed to give Georgia to him? Was her death really approaching that quickly? Was he preparing us for something even more tragic?

The following night, we discovered the answers to these questions.

July 3, 2012, was by far our worst night—definitely Georgia's worst night of seizures. But something was different inside Julia and me. When we heard the first strange breaths coming through the monitor, we didn't panic. Rather than feeling a sense of doom and gloom, we found ourselves calm. Our thoughts were rational as we ran to Georgia's room.

The seizures seemed to be coming more frequently than they had on other nights, so we decided to time them to see exactly how serious the situation was. We prayed for her as she shook all over.

Her body convulsed. Her eyes rolled to the back of her head.

And then it stopped, and Georgia's body became almost as stiff as a board. Her eyes suddenly snapped back into place. She began to blink and look around.

She made a small noise of pain. She did this sometimes, but often there was nothing, no sound coming from her despite having gone through a trauma.

"How long was that one?" I asked Julia, who was eyeing the timer on her phone.

"Five minutes."

They had never lasted that long before. The longest we had experienced up to that point was maybe two minutes, and that was rounding up! This one was a whole three minutes longer. Before we could wrap our heads around this, the whole cycle began again.

Another seizure lasted about five minutes, coming only thirty seconds after the last one. And they kept coming. They were constant and long, and Georgia looked absolutely exhausted.

When this continued for a few hours, we decided to call 911.

"Hi, my daughter has lissencephaly and has been having more seizures than usual tonight. She's been having them for a long time."

Julia's voice was controlled, almost relaxed. The woman I'd known to blast the baby monitor with anxiety was no longer there. She was replaced by a woman calmly doing everything within her control to help her daughter. There was no reason to panic about the rest.

Still, things get very real when an ambulance and fire truck park outside your house. Suddenly you realize how tragic your circumstances are when a firefighter is asking you questions in the living room at three o'clock in the morning. Georgia's situation was no longer hypothetical. As I did my best to answer their questions and watched them hook Georgia up to equipment, it was clear to me that this was far above anything I could help my daughter with.

As a father, I want to provide for and take care of my family. I want to have the answers and protect my wife and daughter when they need me. But as the many uniformed men and women hustled through my house, all I could do was thank God. Thank him for the peace he somehow supernaturally gave me in that moment, thank him for a wife who always had the answer to the question, "What should we do?" and thank him for the friends and family who were walking through all of this with us.

That night, Julia talked to Georgia's neurologist and told him what had been happening. He advised her to increase the dosage of Georgia's seizure medication. There was no need to take her to the ER. The thing is, when the seizures had first started a few months back, we had discovered this medicine was bittersweet. While it helped relieve the seizures, it also took away the personality Georgia had.

Because of her disorder, Georgia was not developing. She couldn't grab onto our fingers or hold up her head, and she barely made eye contact. But there was still someone in there. You caught a glimpse of that someone every now and then. You'd see her when she kicked or when she'd make a fun sound if you sang to her. She had facial expressions and would usually react in some way by moving her head around when you talked to her. But the seizure medication made Georgia seem lifeless.

It was always a hard choice to increase the dosage, but in this moment there really wasn't another option. We gave her more, and the seizures went away for the night. The paramedics and firefighters eventually left. It seemed that July 3 wasn't "the night." Georgia's time was not up. The Veaches were going to live to see another day!

And that day happened to be the Fourth of July. At 7:30 a.m., my mom and dad showed up at our front door. They had come to pray with us and help out with Georgia while we prepared for the outreach occurring that day.

Amid our drama, we had almost forgotten about City Blast. I was suddenly a little panicked that I would now be running a basketball tournament and six miles on zero sleep. But I tried not to let it show.

As we got ready, Julia was torn about whether she should be doing the City Blast thing. After the seizures of the previous night, she felt she needed to be with Georgia. I asked her if I should stay behind, too, and we went back and forth on the point until we heard a new sound.

It wasn't shortness of breath or the small noise that comes at the end of a seizure. It was the sound of choking. That was just what we needed. We both sprinted to the scene. Maybe we were ready for the 10K after all.

With the best of intentions, my mom had fed Georgia a

pureed banana. In the middle of the feeding, Georgia had another seizure. Her body shook all over, the banana lodged in her throat.

Julia ran to our daughter, whose face was now a bright shade of purple. She propped her up and began pounding on her back. I watched as my wife went into superhero mode yet again and performed the Heimlich on our seven-month-old. Out flew the banana.

Georgia didn't quite recover from the breakfast incident, and the seizures started up again. At around eleven that morning, we rushed her to Urgent Care. The clinicians gave her a sedative to calm her down from the chaos of the day, and our baby girl went into a peaceful sleep.

Obviously, we canceled our plans for City Blast. Our pastor found someone else to run the tournament. We told ourselves there'd be more 10K races next year.

- Canceled plans.
- Calls to 911.
- Life-or-death choking.
- Seizures followed by spasms followed by more seizures.
- Late-night calls to the neurologist.
- Trips to Urgent Care.

This was our new life, a violent storm of worst-case scenarios. And we had to learn how to navigate these storms. The week of the Fourth of July made one thing incredibly clear to me. I wasn't discovering that my life was terrible or my situation was desperate and impossible. Though these thoughts occasionally ran through my head, one thing was clear: there was no way we could get through any of this without God. It was out of our control and completely in his.

And perhaps that has been one of the most amazing things about this struggle and all this pain. Somehow, amid it all, I've learned more and more about God. In these painful moments of my life when others have looked up at the heavens, cursed, and asked, "Why, God? How could you?!" I've strangely started to learn more about him. Do I know the purpose for every struggle and hardship? No. But that doesn't mean I can't find him through it all.

Somehow he has snuck in, and I see him in the texts of loved ones, in the support of my community, in my daughter's eyes, in my wife's strength, in the stories of others, and in the late-night conversations when hope seems lost.

Through this pain, I've found God everywhere and have discovered something completely unreasonable. Despite how things may seem, hope is possible even in the most impossible of circumstances.

Chapter One

COMES ALONGSIDE

HAVE YOU EVER READ A QUOTE OR STORY THAT AT ONE TIME had very little relevance to you, but then suddenly clicked in another moment? You might've shouted an automatic "Amen!" during a church service or double tapped an Instagram photo without truly feeling anything inside, but for some reason—in this moment—the words move you in ways they didn't the first time. I'm always fascinated by how words seem to shift and change in their meaning depending on what point in your life you read them.

The word *lissencephaly*, for instance, once had zero meaning for me. It just sounded like random letters doctors used to describe a disease I'd never have to worry about. Today, however, I hear that word, and my mind fills with a very specific image of my daughter and our struggle.

The words of Paul in 2 Corinthians 1:3–5 have had a similar shifting effect for me.

At one time, they were words I "Amen"ed from my seat when a pastor got fired up from the pulpit about facing storms in our lives. Paul wrote powerfully about living through difficult situations and finding the purpose behind our pain. And though these words are beautiful and true, I always had a hard time fully grasping them.

In those verses, Paul says:

He comes alongside us when we go through hard times, and before you know it, he brings us alongside someone else who is going through hard times so that we can be there for that person like God was there for us. We have plenty of hard times that come from following the Messiah, but no more so than the good times of his healing comfort—we get a full measure of that, too. (THE MESSAGE)

When I heard, read, and studied these words previously, I had experienced the "good times" but never endured the "plenty of hard times" that Paul describes. That was until the dreams and visions I had for my family were dashed.

THE DREAM

It's gonna be a boy. I can't wait to find out about my boy! We're gonna play ball together. We're gonna do life together.

These thoughts ran through my head as we drove to our ultrasound. Julia and I were both so confident that a baby boy was inside her tummy. In our minds, we were simply driving to the hospital to get confirmation and go home. We had stayed up late, talking about this boy of ours and planning our future adventures with him.

We saw ourselves at sporting events in high school. We imagined roughhousing with him. In our minds, he was tall, strapping, and the oldest sibling, looking out for the others.

I remember Julia asking me questions such as, "Okay, if it's a boy, what do you think he'll be like?" I would follow this with an hour-long speech, detailing accounts of his life. I could picture it down to the minute. "So I pick him up from school, and he looks over at me like, 'What's up, Dad?' And then we go shoot hoops in the driveway."

"All right, and if it's a girl?" Julia would ask after I finished my monologue.

Nothing. Silence. My mind went blank. "It's not a girl," I'd answer.
"It's a girl!" said the ultrasound technician, and Julia and I froze.
"Do you want to check that again maybe?" I asked.

The technician stared at me. I'm not sure if she'd ever heard that
come out of a father's mouth before. She looked at me like I was a
terrible human being. She was probably right.

"Uh, no. It's a girl," she finally replied matter-of-factly.

Needless to say, we were both shocked by the news. Looking
back at the whole scenario now, I see our reaction was a little silly.
I mean, it's as if we didn't realize there was a 50 percent chance or
something.

As the idea sank in more and more in the weeks following, our
imaginations ran wild with our girl's life, just as they had with the
life of our future son.

Who will this little lady be? we wondered.

The news of your first kid is followed by giant hopes and
dreams. Julia and I soon found ourselves awake at night imagining
this little girl.

First we'd picture taking her for walks in the park. Then we'd
imagine her cuddling with us on the couch. Soon we could see ourselves giving in when she begged us to watch a Disney musical for the
eightieth time and dealing with her attitude in middle school. Next
we envisioned ourselves embarrassing her on her first day of high
school and freaking out about the thought of her getting a driver's
license. This was followed by the anticipation of college graduation
and visions of walking her down the aisle. Then she's a pro volleyball
player! She's winning a gold medal! She's solving world hunger!

When it's your first, it's easy to get carried away.

Any parent could tell you that with a new life comes a whole
lot of expectation. And when it came to our daughter, my wife and I
were no different.

Yes, we joked about making sure our daughter became a college athlete or had her mother's beauty and her father's legs. (Yes, I have some very nice legs, okay? Don't worry about it.) We laughed and dreamed up some crazy plans for Georgia, but we also had serious hopes for her life.

I remember my dad telling me about when my mom was pregnant with me, and how they, too, experienced this first-time-parent dreaming. He told me how he prayed over my mom's belly. Full of nerves about what was to come and how he was going to raise me, he prayed for God's help. He also prayed that God's will—his plan, his purpose, and his destiny—would be done in my life.

It was even before Julia and I got pregnant that my dad told me about these prayers. "Chad, I have watched everything I've prayed come to pass in your life," he said. "I asked God to do these amazing things for you, and he's done them all."

Like father, like son. Inspired by this story and wanting to follow in the old man's footsteps, I decided that I, too, would pray over my daughter before she ever arrived.

"God, give her a global grace."

For some reason, this was the prayer that always came out as I laid hands on Julia's stomach. I would imagine my daughter's life on this massive scale.

"Let her be used for your glory around the world." The world. Millions of people. Influence. These were the prayers I felt I was supposed to pray over our girl.

I asked this every night with my hands on Julia's belly, not quite sure why I prayed that prayer but believing that something about our girl would have an impact around the world.

And I kept praying.

I thought that maybe when Georgia was a young adult or even later in her life this prayer I had for her would become a reality. Perhaps she'd travel and do ministry like good ol' Dad. Maybe she'd become famous for acting or inventing and have an amazing platform. I pictured her doing TED talks at the age of twenty-eight or signing the cover of her life-changing book around the world. I had a feeling Georgia was going to affect people and make them think—make them think about God, even.

Never in my wildest dreams would I have believed she would be doing this, impacting the world, by four months old.

Never in my wildest dreams would I have believed the reason.

Oh, Jo

Let me tell you about another dreamer found in the Bible named Joseph. At seventeen years old, Jo could *dream*. He wasn't one of those young people who failed to set goals or make five-year plans. In his mind, his future was much more than living off of his parents and working two shifts a week at the local coffee stand.

Jo saw himself thriving. God gave him dreams and visions of his future self, ruling over his brothers and entire family. When he went to bed at night, he saw images of power and authority and, controversially, his brothers bowing down before him. Genesis 37 describes how Joseph decided to tell his brothers about these little visions. I wasn't there, but I can imagine it was probably an awkward conversation.

"Yeah, so you guys are all going to bow to me one day! Pretty sick, huh?" There's really no hope that a statement like that will go over well. And in Genesis 37:5 it says, "When he told it to his brothers, they hated him all the more."

But all this hatred didn't stop Jo from dreaming, and despite how well his last dream play-by-play went with his siblings, he had another dream and decided to share it yet again. And yet again, it involved them bowing and him ruling.

His brothers might not have liked it, but God was the one giving these visions to Jo. Like the "she will have a global grace" cry I felt so strongly about Georgia, Joseph knew he would one day have incredible influence.

How he would attain that influence and the journey he would travel to get there, however, he most likely did not expect. If anyone can relate to the struggle that comes with this life, it's him. After being sold into slavery by his brothers who hated him, then being thrown into jail for doing absolutely nothing wrong, Joseph's dreams were dashed again and again. And oh, can I relate.

"She Will Never"

My mom was the first one to say something. Though we also may have noticed how something was not quite right, my wife and I immediately took the defensive. After all, this was our daughter—the only kid we'd ever had. Not even Momma was going to mess with that. Yes, we noticed Georgia wasn't the best at grasping tightly onto our fingers. We also knew she had always been an easy baby. She wouldn't cry when she woke up; she wouldn't cry when she was hungry. She rarely ever cried, in fact. We thought we were lucky and blessed with a very sweet, calm kid.

But another month went by, and we could no longer deny that something was a little off. Georgia's eyes didn't seem to focus on us when we talked to her, and they sometimes went crossed. The twitch in her eye concerned us more than her not crying. Maybe because it didn't look like something we could write off as part of her personality.

Something was wrong.

We updated our church and our close friends and family to let them know we were going for a checkup to see if everything was all right. "There might be something wrong with Georgia's eyesight. If you could pray with us, that'd be amazing!"

When it was time to go to the doctor's appointment for that first exam, we had already sent out many positive mass texts and had a ton of people standing by, praying for a good report. Our church and friends were full of faith, and we were getting constant texts from them:

"Believing that her vision will be perfect!"

"God is able! Praying for Georgia today and for a good report!"

There was a positive anthem beating inside us from all the support. So as we walked through the doors of the clinic, we didn't even consider hearing anything negative, in much the same way that Joseph didn't consider doing anything but declaring his amazing dreams to his brothers.

But that first checkup led to another checkup, which led to another, and another, until . . .

April 10, 2012, the day I realized exactly what Paul meant by "plenty of hard times."

We sat down to get the diagnosis from the doctor and could feel "it" instantly. If you've ever experienced a traumatic event or heard bad news, you know which "it" I'm talking about. The tone in the doctor's voice, the pace with which he spoke, and his body language all hinted that Julia and I needed to brace ourselves.

Cancer? A rare blood disease? What was our baby girl going to face? Whatever it was, God would be there with us through it all. Julia and I could deal with this. We could fight whatever sickness the enemy had planned. Our friends were standing by, waiting for a text message, and we were ready to respond with good Christian faith and texts that read:

"God is good. We're going to fight this!"

"By his stripes we are healed!"

"God came that we might enjoy life and life more abundantly!"

And then the doctor started talking, and all the noise was sucked out of the room. The world seemed to stop.

"Your daughter has lissencephaly."

As I mentioned, this word was gibberish to me and to Julia. For all we knew, it could have meant anything from a rare form of cancer to a mild sore throat. But nothing could have prepared me for what he said next.

"Lissencephaly is often referred to as 'smooth brain.'"

Smooth brain. This does not sound good, I thought. And I was right.

"She will never develop past three months. She will never walk. She will never talk. She will never roll over. She will never crawl . . ."

A few more *nevers* in, and everything started moving very slowly. Suddenly, those scriptures weren't popping up in my mind. I wasn't able to smile my typical grin of faith. My heart dropped to my socks as my wife started weeping beside me. I was shocked.

We buckled Georgia into her car seat and didn't talk the whole way home. Our phones were blowing up with questions. "What did the doctor say?" and "How'd it go?" But we couldn't text back. We faced forward and drove, trying to process the doctor's words.

It was worse than we had anticipated. Our daughter didn't need glasses because of her eyes. She didn't need medicine to help her cry more or squeeze our fingers more tightly.

Our daughter's brain didn't work.

The hopes and plans we had made for her future suddenly left an ache in our hearts. We felt like Joseph, imagining a bright future but facing the reality of slavery. Looking back at that moment, one scripture ultimately stands out above the others.

Proverbs 13:12 says, "Hope deferred makes the heart sick."

It's a perfect way to describe that ride home and the feeling in my gut.

I felt *sick.*

There I was, someone who had preached God's goodness from the platform, someone who knew all the verses and all the right things to say, suddenly facing the stark reality of Paul's words in 2 Corinthians. I was, for the first time, truly realizing that my life wasn't free of harm. Just as so many of the heroes I had read about in the Bible had gone through trials and storms and "hard times," I, too, had to face them. Not just Joseph, but Jacob, Moses, Job, Daniel, Rahab, Jonah—the list of people in the Bible who encountered terrible trials goes on.

Why have I always failed to realize what was actually happening to these people in these stories? I wondered. It seemed I had thought life would be all butterflies and daisies. But when "smooth brain" entered my life, I realized that pain was real and actually a part of life.

Posting #thestruggleisreal may be a silly joke we use when the line at Starbucks is too long or we can't seem to find the perfect new outfit for our next big event. We use it when laughing at life's first-world problems or things that make us upset even though they're petty. But struggle really *is* a part of this life. Little, insignificant things bring us down every day for no reason, but most of us will also experience the huge, very significant pain that comes with simply living on this earth. April 10, 2012, was the first time I experienced that level of pain.

"So That We Can Be There"

During the aftermath of Diagnosis Day, I was still a pastor. People still expected me to have answers. And with Georgia's disorder came a multitude of questions. People were ready for the life lesson in this terrible circumstance.

"What's God's purpose in all of this?"

"Do you believe Georgia will be healed?"

"Why do you think this happened to you?"

These are only a few of the many questions that have come my way since Diagnosis Day.

This book is my best attempt at an answer. My goal is not to provide the perfect recipe for grief, the formula for getting the healing you've been waiting for, or the answer to the philosophical questions regarding why God lets us suffer. Rather, it's to offer hope, however unreasonable it may seem, and to point you to the one who comforts.

I have experienced the God who truly surrounds me and is near me as I face life's most difficult circumstances. I hope, through my story, you will see the countless ways he's come through for my family. And why? Why has he come through for us over and over again? I believe he's done all this for Julia and me, so we can be there for that person who is hurting—be there the way God was there for us. Throughout this life, I've been surrounded by countless people who need this very thing; however, I'm embarrassed to admit my response has not always been the best.

As I've mentioned, before my dreams for Georgia and my family were ripped from me, my reality was pretty much free from pain. I remember seeing others experiencing terrible sickness or circumstances and having a hard time relating to them and coming alongside them with true sorrow for their situation. One instance in particular sticks out in my mind. It's difficult to mention without feeling a wave of regret, but here goes . . .

I've known my sister Bethany's husband, Marc, since he was twenty-one, vibrant and full of life. Over a period of time, I watched Marc's lifestyle be turned completely upside down. His body began to deteriorate because he suffered from diabetes.

Pneumonia for three months here.

Kidney transplant there.

I was on the sidelines as he went to the hospital again and again. This seemed to be a day in the life for Marc.

"Oh, Marc, can't go play golf? Man, that sucks."

I'm embarrassed to say that this was about the extent of my response to my brother's suffering. I wasn't aching inside. I felt very removed from his pain just as I had felt removed from Paul's words to the Corinthians. *Yeah, bad things happen. I get it.*

But I was far from getting it.

It was something I viewed from a distance, as if looking through a foggy window. I'd hear about Marc's latest doctor's visit and think, *That's really too bad.* Did I feel bummed out that my sister and her family had to go through all this? Yes. But, I'm ashamed to admit, that was about all I felt. I got bummed out. I felt a little sad. I said things like, "Poor Marc and Bethany." Then I went on with the rest of my day.

But after Diagnosis Day, Julia and I were suddenly the ones going to the hospital . . . again and again.

An MRI here.

A feeding tube there.

Needless to say, my perspective and heart for my brother-in-law's situation shifted dramatically. The reality of medical bills and the exhausting life that Marc and my sister had been living sank in during the months following April. The indifference I once felt about Marc's situation, the feeling of being removed from his pain and not understanding exactly how bad it was, soon was replaced by an overwhelming empathy.

No longer was it, "Oh, that's just the way it is for Marc." Instead, I was ready to do battle, to pray, and to believe for something better! Because of our situation with Georgia, I started to understand that a life of diabetes and constant doctors' care was not the life God had in mind for Marc.

Empathy.

It's a powerful emotion that has nothing to do with you but everything to do with other people. When you've gone through something tragic and have seen God come and stand beside you, all you want is to do the same for others. *Lightbulb!*

I discovered my newfound empathy revealing itself in other situations, as I began to see struggle all around. Last year, Austin, a groomsman in my wedding and one of my closest friends, was faced with his own terrible situation. Like Julia's and mine, it involved the life of his child. He and his wife, Emily, were pregnant and found out four months into the pregnancy that their baby's organs were not developing. The doctors claimed their son had no chance of surviving birth. When they received this news, Austin and Emily decided to leave their jobs and their lives in LA to move home to Washington. They wanted to be close to family as they faced this giant and believed for a miracle.

I'll never forget the day I got the call that Madden had been born. I was told Austin and Emily's little boy lived only a few seconds before passing. The miracle did not happen, and my friend had to face what no person should ever have to face.

When we heard the news, Julia and I immediately rushed to the hospital to be with them in their worst hour, hold little Madden, and say good-bye.

As I walked into the hospital room, I felt the same sickness that I had two years earlier when we received Georgia's diagnosis. My heart broke for Austin, who, too, was forced to see his dreams and hopes for his child deferred. Sorrow came over me as I entered that room. Perhaps if Madden had died before Georgia's diagnosis, I would have been sad. I may have even cried. But there was something different about the emotion that overtook me that day.

Though the process is still ongoing with Georgia three years later, and though she still has multiple seizures throughout the day, I have truly known the God who comes alongside me that Paul mentions in 2 Corinthians. It has been my greatest joy to stand with those who encounter storms, to pass them that fresh glass of water with empathy and hope. For years I've been able to rejoice with those who rejoice. But I now truly know what it means to mourn with those who mourn.

THE REALITY

Why did Austin's baby die while other babies come into this world happy and healthy? Why is Georgia's brain not developing while other kids her age and younger start to walk and talk? The truth is that life isn't about comparing how much worse one situation is from another. Rather, it's about standing alongside others as they experience life's ups and downs.

Pain is relative, and Jesus is a reality.

As I mentioned, I'm not here to teach about how to get healed and why God heals some and not others. Though I do believe that God is able and desires to heal all, my focus is not on the what or the how of Christianity but on the *who*.

So here I am, eager to come alongside you and reveal the one who came alongside me. I know what it feels like to face life's cruel blows and what it is to search for the perfect reaction and response when everything crumbles around you. I hope that as I share the journey my wife and I have taken, our failures and successes, you'll realize that Jesus is all that matters and he has a purpose for you, even in all this pain.

Ultimately, this is not a sad book about a three-year-old with a brain disorder no one can pronounce. It's not a book about a pastor's struggle to cope. It's not about bitterness, panic, depression, or fear, though all of these are definitely part of our story. It's a book about the Provider, the Protector, and the One who is with us in the midst of the storm. The *who* behind it all.

It's about Jesus, the one God wants to point people to. Despite pain and circumstances, God will find a way to reveal his Son to us. Sometimes he will even use tragedy to show us how he can triumph. Our situation with Georgia is no exception. When you're asking "Why?" just as I have asked so many times, I hope that you, too, will find this Jesus who desperately wants to walk with you through whatever may come.

Chapter Two

FORGETFUL JONES

GOD IS SO GOOD.

I know this because he gives us words like *Bro, Homie, Dude,* and *Playa.* This exhaustive list of creative non-names is just resting in our back pockets, waiting for us to pull it out when we find ourselves in *that* moment: the moment when we've forgotten a person's actual name.

"Hey . . ."

We've all been there with blank minds, standing in front a person we've had countless conversations with, searching our brains.

Okay, I got this. I'll just start with the As. Allen, Adam, Andrew, Anayayaya . . . Alexis? Can that be a boy's name too? No, there's no time for that! I'll just go with . . .

". . . you."

And he knows. And you know. You're not getting out of this one.

"It's Ben."

Why did I stop after the As, Lord?!

Forgetting is the worst. Scanning the dark caverns of a blank mind can lead to heart-thumping, forehead-sweating panic.

However, forgetting a name is only a small taste of true panic. It's there and oh-so-real, but moments later we're shaking it off like Taylor Swift.

A slightly bigger taste of panic comes when we lose the small device that carries our entire lives—our cell phones.

We pat our pockets.

We pat our sleeves.

We pat our shins. (Why do we do that? There's nothing in our shins!)

We assume the worst. We're imagining it on top of the car, flying down the freeway to an ungodly doom! Or has it become a new chew toy for our sister's pet dog? We freak out as we sherlock our way through the mystery of this precious part of our lives.

I've experienced this particular brand of panic on more than one occasion. So when I see another endure it, my heart goes out to him. This happened one day at the airport, while going through security with my friend. I had brought him along on a speaking trip so that he could play worship.

Today, walking through security is an accomplishment. In the nineties you could stroll right in as if you owned the place and greet your friends as they came off the plane! Now you have to follow a giant checklist:

Shoes off: *check.*

Laptop out: *check.*

Liquids in a separate baggy: *check.*

Going through security feels like a full-time job. And this time was no different. My friend and I were ready to get through, put our hands above our heads, have our creepy pictures taken, get our coffee, and park with a magazine at the gate until our flight took off.

After we finally we made it through, we high-fived each other and cheered, super pumped at our huge life accomplishment. "We did it! We're free!" Then we headed over to the gate.

As we walked through to board the plane, my friend stopped dead in his tracks, his eyes huge. He looked as if he had just seen a ghost.

"Bro, you okay?" I asked. I wasn't sure if he was going to throw up.

"I think I forgot my . . . *phone.*"

At that moment, something came over me. It was an adrenaline that I think only soldiers can understand. My brother had left his phone behind. In true *Saving Private Ryan* fashion, I looked at him and yelled, "Your phone?! *Runnnnn! Run, man, run!* For I will stay. And, I will pray." And off he ran, almost in slow motion, to the security check-in, his life on the line. My heart raced as I prayed, "Lord, not today. Today is *not* the day that he loses his phone. Not on my watch, God!"

And I'm happy to report that this war story has a happy ending. The phone was found. All was well in the world.

We all hate forgetting something important, hate that moment when our eyes widen and we realize what we've left behind; but the real panic doesn't come from lost phones, wallets, or names. It comes when we start forgetting about someone far more crucial to our survival.

What happens when we forget about God?

Paul said in Philippians 4:8, "Whatever is true, whatever is noble, whatever is right, whatever is pure, whatever is lovely, whatever is admirable—if anything is excellent or praiseworthy—think about such things."

Forgetting a name may cost you an awkward moment. Forgetting your phone may cost you a trip to the Apple store and the loss of a few texts you thought were more important than they actually are. But how much does forgetting about God cost you? What does it cost when your mind isn't filled with who God is, what he's done, and other praiseworthy, lovely things?

There are certain things we should not forget.

The Storm

When I read about the disciples on a boat with a storm crashing around them, I can't help but imagine they had forgotten the most important thing. I imagine Peter and the rest of the team completely freaking out on the boat. I see them saying things like, "We're all going to die if we don't do something!"

Matthew 8:24 says, "Suddenly a furious storm came up on the lake, so that the waves swept over the boat. But Jesus was sleeping."

I don't know about you, but "furious" doesn't sound too good. Jesus, the all-powerful Son of God, would obviously be the best person to wake up at this terrifying moment. But imagine how the disciples felt. I mean, he was asleep. Jesus! The guy who was constantly ministering and probably exhausted. He most likely needed his rest.

Were I one of the disciples, I would've played Rock, Paper, Scissors to see who had to wake him up to ask for help. What better way to solve a life-or-death situation? The Bible doesn't say who the lucky loser of this game was, the one who finally did the waking up, but I like to think it was Peter. He tends to play major roles in other boat-related Bible stories, so let's go with him.

Here's how I imagine it played out . . .

Peter ran over to the corner of the boat where his teacher lay peacefully, nestled in blankets. Rain beat down on him, and the wind tossed waves of water onto his blanket. *How is he sleeping through this?* Peter probably thought.

Peter was nervous to disrupt his master's sleep no matter how ridiculous it seemed. He wondered what name he should use when he tapped him awake. I mean, how would *you* wake up Jesus?

Prince of peace? Nah. Too cheesy. King of kings? No, maybe Lord of lords. Oh, Son of Man. That's it! I'll go with Son of Man.

Before he could even utter these words with a light, gentle tap, a giant gust of wind blew and knocked Peter off his feet. He looked at his friends as they desperately tried to keep water out of the boat. One was clinging to the boat, literally holding on for dear life. Peter panicked.

"You have to save us or we're going to drown!"

He was shocked at how the scream boomed out of him. Desperation made his voice crack uncomfortably.

The young, sleeping teacher popped awake in an instant. He looked at Peter with the you-did-not-just-wake-me-up-from-a-nap face. (We've all made this face. Everyone needs a good five-minute grace period after they wake up.) Then Jesus calmly rose to see what the fuss was about.

Peter couldn't believe it. Even now that Jesus was awake and could take in their dire circumstances, he still seemed unfazed that his life was in jeopardy. All their lives were.

"Do something, or this is all over!" Peter yelled again.

The calm teacher walked forward, as if not listening. He shook his head, looking at the chaos.

"Why are you freaking out, Peter? Do you have *any* faith at all?"

He turned to the water, wind beating against his hair and his robe. The storm was so loud and the rain so hard that Peter could barely make out everything that was happening. Three of the guys were still frantically trying to keep the water out. More had joined in clinging to the boat as it rocked back and forth. But Jesus just stood in the center of it all.

"Stop!" he said.

And all went calm.

SEIZURE SUMMER

As I've mentioned, after Diagnosis Day, Julia and I were overwhelmed by the support and community that came around us. "God can do all things!" "We believe she will be healed!" "We pray for Georgia every day!" The love of family and friends and even strangers was incredible.

The initial shock hit us hard, but this support provided us an unexpected confidence. I've heard it said before that "you can face anything in life, as long as you don't face it alone." This was the first time I experienced it. There's something about community and faith that make you stand a little taller and smile in the face of adversity. People surrounded us and filled us with more confidence every day. We were ready for God to come through as he'd done for so many before us.

We got this, I thought. *God is so big. Who are you, doctors? How can you say never? She will. Through Christ, she can!*

We had read again and again a stack of papers that detailed everything we should expect from the monster of lissencephaly. Some of these included "unusual facial appearance," "difficulty swallowing," "muscle spasms," and "severe psychomotor retardation." Such wonderful words to speak over your family. Not.

And Googling the name of the disorder was even worse. We'd type in those thirteen awful letters and see image after image of disabled kids and horror stories. Tales of children dying way before their time, images of kids drooling in wheelchairs—these all made us close our laptops fast.

Yet even though these predictions were ugly and difficult to read or look at, somehow they were still only that—predictions. Nothing *had* happened yet. Georgia was a beautiful baby with perfect little features. There was no "unusual facial appearance" here, thank you very much. Somehow that made hope for tomorrow a bit easier.

Then Seizure Summer came. Julia was driving to church with Georgia in the car seat when the first one happened. As I've mentioned, it was about a month and a half after her diagnosis. Georgia's body went stiff, and she stared off into nothingness. This was followed by a series of spasms and shakes. Julia called me while I was in the church service, her voice shaking as she recounted the event.

Soon Georgia's seizures became more frequent and more violent. By the end of the summer, our girl was having them up to fifty times a day. That's two seizures an hour! Her symptoms were no longer words on paper. Lissencephaly became much more real.

One night during that summer after the Fourth of July, Julia was out running errands, most likely taking a break from the constant seizure maintenance. Georgia lay on her back in our bed, those blue eyes looking around again, and I sat with her, looking into them.

When I looked at Georgia, I couldn't help but think how she was such a beautiful, breathtaking baby. Dark, wild hair like her parents', big eyes, a perfect little button nose. It was common for people to walk up to us on the street, not knowing she was sick, and admire how cute she was. For Julia and me, this was always a breath of fresh air. People treated Georgia normally, without any worry in their eyes about her disorder. It was nice just to celebrate her beauty with a stranger.

Then another seizure started. I knew it was coming, because I saw it in her eyes. It always started in her eyes. They no longer looked around but glossed over and rolled to the back of her head. Then her entire body tightened. After a few moments, she snapped out of it and the tremors began. She shook in the aftermath of the seizure. The whole thing looked so traumatic and painful and, worst of all, there was nothing I could do.

God, I need you so badly. There doesn't seem to be any solution but waiting it out. Do I have to sit here and endure this? Do I have to stand by and watch my child experience this pain? Are Julia and I destined to be simply caretakers? We want to be parents, God, not nurses! This hurts. Please, God. Please, make this stop!

God is not afraid of our vulnerability. He's not afraid when we come to him with transparency and lay all our pain down for him to work out. In my desperate dad state, I wasn't afraid to tell him all about it.

But at that moment, I was having a hard time recalling all that God had already done for me. All I could see was how absolutely negative and dark my circumstance was. The faith that had built up since the diagnosis was suddenly hard to find. Like the disciples in the storm, I felt alone and started to panic.

THE DEVIL'S PLAYGROUND

At first glance, the disciples' boat trip is a strange story. If Jesus, the Son of God, is on your boat, everything should be easy, right? God is on your side and literally *by* your side when you're a disciple. But just because Jesus is with you doesn't mean you're free from trials. Storms still happen when you know and love God. But how does God want us to respond to these storms?

Fear happens when we leave our minds empty. This is where the devil, evil thoughts, panic, and confusion take over. The enemy has a free playground upon which to roam and do as he pleases. Jesus was right there with the disciples, and still they had little faith that they would survive the storm.

Our human response when everything hits the fan is typically to forget who we have in our boat with us.

In looking back on Seizure Summer, I know that Jesus was by my side. The same Jesus who'd set me free as a teenager, the same God who'd rescued and comforted me time and time again, the same Jesus who'd surrounded me with support and community when Julia and I got the diagnosis. I knew he was there, and yet, in that moment, my mind was empty.

Like the disciples, I was blanking and failing to realize who I had with me. I let the terror of watching my daughter helplessly endure her thousandth-something seizure cause me to forget the God who can stop the storm.

So what are we to do in life's seemingly impossible situations? Remember.

This is the journey I've been on. It's one that involves practicing remembrance. I need to remember my story, what Jesus has done for me. I need to remember the Bible's story, what Jesus has done for the world.

All throughout this good book, God asks his people to remember. Even the children of Israel, who were taken out of Egypt and slavery, panicked in the wilderness. God had used miracle after miracle to free them from the hands of an evil leader, and yet, once they were out and free, they saw no food around them and were alarmed.

"If only we would've died by the Lord's hand in Egypt!" they said, like a bunch of whiners. "At least in Egypt there was food!" (Ex. 16).

And the panic didn't end there. First they worried that they'd be in slavery forever. God freed them. Then they worried that they'd starve to death. God fed them. Over and over again, they grumbled and freaked out, continually forgetting all that God had done for them. Because of this forgetfulness, the Israelites thought their situation was the absolute worst.

During this time, God called his people to remember. He spoke to Moses, as he often did throughout this story, and told him to remind the people who had freed them, who had parted the Red Sea, who had come through for them time and time again.

"Mo!" God said to him before he handed him the Ten Commandments. "You go down there, and you tell the people everything I did for them. You remind them that I'm the God who brought them out of Egypt. *Egypt!* I don't know if they remember that place, but it wasn't pretty. There was slavery and the murder of children happening there. Now they're talking about going back? Now they're complaining? You go down there and remind them that I'm the God who put the cloud up during the day and the night. I'm the God who brought them manna when they were hungry and put shoes on their feet. You remind them, Mo. You tell them what's up."

He wanted them to remember.

If we believe life is about avoiding all trouble, living with no pain, or taking an easy "walk in the park," we're missing what God has for us. He never promised us a safe journey, only a safe arrival. Did he claim "Ye shall have a life without trials, tribulations, and hardships. Thus saith the Lord"? No! But he did promise that he would be by our side "to the very end of the age" (Matt. 28:20).

As we look throughout the Bible, we can see people like David who were confident in this. David was the king of Israel, who walked through his own terrible trials. He endured King Saul, his mentor, wanting him dead. His own son betrayed him. He made massive mistakes that involved lust and adultery. Life was not always easy for David. And yet, he has gone down in history for his praise songs to God. He's known for the way he remembered and thanked God for all he'd done for him. His book is one of the most popular in the Bible—the book of Psalms. If you've never stepped foot in a church building, you've most likely heard these psalms at funerals or weddings.

One of these songs goes a little something like this: "Yea, though I walk through the valley of the shadow of death, I will fear no evil; for You are with me; Your rod and Your staff, they comfort me" (Ps. 23:4 NKJV). You may be wondering who Rod is and why he needs a whole staff of people to comfort David, but don't let that sidetrack you from David's real point here. He's saying, "If I have God with me, I don't need to be afraid of anything life throws my way." (Oh, and Google "shepherd terms." It may help you understand the Bible.)

God has an amazing journey in store for us. But to know where we're going next, we can't forget where we've been. The truth is that nothing is too difficult for God. In trouble, this is what we must cling to. In the "shadow of death" and brain disorders, this is where we must look.

Chapter Three

DAUGHTER NAMED RUTH

A *SLAM* MAGAZINE WAS OPENED ON MY NIGHTSTAND TO AN image of Jordan dunking over a struggling Bob Sura—the *slam-a-da-month*. When your life revolves around basketball, these are the things that wake you up in the morning.

That and the fifteen basketball posters you have hanging around your room, the two pairs of Air Jordans you have sitting in your closet, and the knee-high socks you wear to hide your skinny legs. The ones you have to tape up because Nike doesn't make them in men's petite.

This is how I started the basketball season of my senior year in high school, 1998. I had been playing as shooting guard on a basketball team since middle school with all my closest friends. It was *my* position, and this was going to be *my* year.

After adjusting the tape on my knee-high socks, I walked into the gym as if I ran that town. I was ready for the coach to read off the lineup and start the season.

"Point guard . . . Henry."

I high-fived my buddy, super pumped that we'd get to start this thing together.

"Shooting guard . . ."

I started to gangsta-walk onto the court. *I got this.*

". . . James."

Then I gangsta-walked slowly backward to my seat on the bench. *James? James?!* My mind exploded with shock.

To understand the devastation in my little eighteen-year-old heart, you have to understand that James was the coach's son and a sixteen-year-old sophomore. When you're in your thirties, a two-year age difference means you are basically the same age. When you are a senior in high school, a sixteen-year-old looks like a child you should be babysitting. And here was one of those children, barging in and ripping my hopes and dreams from me, taking *my* position.

I had envisioned my final year of high school going a certain way, and I was robbed of it. I now had to watch another get the glory while I sat on the bench, waiting for my turn.

I was depressed. I was disappointed. But more than anything, I felt a sharp sort of pain that lingered after each game. It followed me all the way home and to the next game and the next. I looked at James, I looked at his dad, and I felt rejected. I was upset with them. And it didn't seem to go away.

It was bitterness.

The ugly sort of anger that comes when circumstances seem unfair. The sort that lingers around for a while, or isn't ever inclined to leave.

THE COMPARING GAME

His laughter was hysterical. One of those deep chuckles that kids get when they're tired and probably should be sleeping. The two-year-old boy, with his giant head of curly hair, used two straws to beat on the restaurant table like a drum. His parents were also in a fit of laughter at their son, who was putting on a concert for the whole restaurant.

Julia leaned over to me. "That's what she's supposed to be doing."

She seemed to have radar that went off when kids the same age as Georgia were nearby. She'd watch them closely with focused eyes.

She'd study their actions and look back and forth from Georgia to them, as if taking notes on the stark differences.

Smiles at parents, she'd jot down in this imaginary notebook.

Excellent motor skills.

Eye contact.

Ability to say two to three words.

Noted.

I usually would try to change the subject to keep her mind off of it. "Babe, this food is so good" or "Babe, do you want to split dessert?" Anything to unlock her eyes from the happy two-year-old playing drums for his proud parents.

But the truth was that I noticed too. This kid was sitting up, laughing, and drumming, and his parents were thrilled. It was obvious that he was the same age and size as Georgia.

I leaned over to the stroller parked next to the table and gave Georgia a kiss on the cheek. She always kicked her feet when I did that and gave an adorable half smile. I tried to focus on her solely, to drown out the rest of the restaurant.

It was one thing to have G all alone to ourselves at the house. There we could celebrate small smiles like these, moments of eye contact, or simply a day without a seizure. (We would throw a giant parade for a day without a seizure!) But when we went out in public and saw other kids crawling, walking, talking, or running, it all felt so unfair.

Holidays were the worst.

The MacGregors (Julia's family) and the Veaches (mine) have had a long tradition of Thanksgivings together, dating back to before Julia and I were even born. Without getting into too many details, the story goes like this:

My dad went to college with her dad.

They got saved together.

They both became pastors around the same time.

Our parents got married on the same day, at the same hour, of the same year.

They became young married couples together and raised kids together.

Because of all this, the Veaches and the MacGregors celebrated Thanksgiving together every year.

Someone once asked me, "Oh, so you guys were like childhood sweethearts?"

But that's not exactly how it went down. I didn't marry my childhood sweetheart or my almost cousin. What happened was . . .

Because of college and living in LA, I missed seven straight Thanksgivings in a row. When I came back to the Thanksgiving table, I looked across and thought to myself, *Dang. Julia done grown up! Please pass the mashed potatoes. Let me get some of that gravy!* And the rest was history.

After marriage and babies, the Veaches and MacGregors continued to gather around the turkey every November. Each Thanksgiving we packed the house with two very loud, crazy groups of people and a ton of kids. Merci, Phoenix, Boston, Scout, Wallace, Ramona, Beckham, Merryweather. The cousins were multiplying and quickly.

An adult table and a kid table were no longer enough. We needed a twenty-four-hour bouncing castle to entertain the many energetic toddlers who ran around the house.

Thanksgiving has always been my wife's favorite holiday, and ever since it became the day I found "the one," I'm also a pretty big fan. But strangely, after Georgia's diagnosis, Julia and I found that the Veach–MacGregor gatherings that had once brought us life and community were suddenly leaving us feeling sad. Even inside a house packed with people and sitting at a table squished with family members, we felt very alone. Each year our nieces and nephews grew before our eyes, forming sentences and some intense personalities. And at every gathering there was Georgia, lying quietly on a blanket that we'd set up for her on the couch or on a sofa cushion, barely taking in the Veach–MacGregor madness.

At home she was the most special part of our day. But during the holidays and the family photos that came with the holidays, we tried desperately for her not to look "special." For a long time, family photos with Georgia were no problem because she was so young and small. We had no real issues for the first six to nine months because she was such a beautiful little baby. She'd sleep in our arms, and we'd snap a beautiful pic of the family. It was a piece of cake. But the older Georgia got, the fact that she had special needs began to show.

It's hard enough to get a solid photo of a group of twenty people (half of them kids), but often we'd take up to fifty photos with everyone only to discover that Georgia was making a strange face in every single one. It was frustrating, and often Julia would plead with everyone to leave Georgia out of the picture. She didn't want to deal with the pain of another photo drawing attention to Georgia's illness. "No, she's part of the family!" or "No, we all need to be in it together!" they'd say, with the best of intentions. They didn't want to exclude Georgia, but they didn't realize how difficult the experience was for us.

After the nightmare of family photos was done, we'd usually sit back with the rest of the family and watch the other little ones having fun. Like any parent, we wanted the same for our daughter.

As we drove away from those family gatherings, a knot formed in both of our stomachs. This knot is a common human feeling when we see others' seemingly better circumstances and wonder why we're sitting on the bench, watching our dreams lived out by someone else.

Panic may have come during the traumatic moments of lissencephaly. But in the quiet moments, the day-to-day, something far more dangerous started to form in us—a hint of bitterness trying to eat away at our spirits. We had to learn to work hard against it, to not let it grow into something that ruined our lives.

We had a lot to learn.

FROM PLEASANT TO BITTER

Let me tell you about a lady in the Bible who had her own set of problems and her own taste of bitterness. We're not just talking about family photos–type problems. We're talking about husband-dead, son-dead, other-son-dead-too type of problems.

This woman's story takes place in the book of Ruth. Since the book is titled "Ruth," you might presume Ruth is the key player of the story; but I've always found Naomi's narrative most interesting. This may be because I've encountered my own fair share of trials lately.

Naomi was a woman whose name meant "pleasant." This is what her parents chose for her. Have you ever noticed that some parents are really, *really* into the meaning of their baby's name?

"Oh, what a cute baby name."

"Yes, it means 'light of the universe.' We prayed about it and felt like yes, that's it. Our child *will* be the light of the universe, you know?"

I remember when people asked us about Georgia's name. "Oh, Georgia. How pretty. Why did you name her that?"

"Because we liked the way it . . . sounded . . . when we said it?" I'd usually reply, confused as to why there would be another reason.

"Well, what does it mean?" they'd ask.

I decided I should probably have a better answer for questions like these, so I did a little Google search.

The meaning of the name Georgia. Enter.

Google answered this way: *Georgia is the feminine version of the name George.*

After that, I decided to stick with "we liked the way it sounded."

I'm not sure if you are aware, but the parents of the Bible days were super into baby name meanings too. They were all about it, and Naomi's folks were no different. They picked a name especially for her.

Pleasant.

But when Naomi found herself in the worst of life circumstances, this name seemed like a cruel joke. *Thanks a lot, Mom and Dad. Here I am, walking around thinking everything's going to be pleasant, thinking I'd live a long life with a husband and see my family grow, have grandbabies, get to retirement. Now look at me!* This is how I imagine Naomi's internal monologue.

When her husband died, her life felt anything but pleasant. She thought she had reached her breaking point, cried every last tear. But life, it seemed, wasn't finished with her yet. What happened next was beyond tears. Her sons, the greatest part of her life, died too. She felt empty and alone.

Despite this tragedy, Naomi managed to journey on. She decided to return to her homeland and leave the scene of her terrible sadness. She intended to take this journey alone, but her daughter-in-law Ruth wanted to go with her. Ruth looked at her and delivered, in my opinion, one of the more cinematic lines in the Bible. I always imagine it being said with an epic score playing in the background.

"Where you go I will go, and where you stay I will stay. Your people will be my people and your God my God" (Ruth 1:16).

Talk about loyalty.

So they began their journey back to Naomi's homeland. *How am I going to look to my old friends?* Naomi wondered as they walked. She began to dread the whole thing as one dreads a high school reunion.

Everybody would run out to meet her, their iPhones filled with photos of their grandbabies and of their kids' college graduations. And what was Naomi bringing with her? Nothing. No grandbabies. Just a sob story about her dead family members.

They probably won't even recognize me, she thought. She knew she wasn't exactly looking her best at the moment. She'd cried for weeks straight, and her eyes were ringed with dark circles. Maybe she could remain incognito.

When she had left her hometown, she was dreamy-eyed with a family and a full life. She had once talked with excitement to her old friends about the future that awaited her. Now she felt embarrassed. She had to come back and tell everyone how things didn't work out as planned.

"Is that it there?" Ruth asked as they arrived at the town.

Her young daughter-in-law should have been tired from such a long journey, but Naomi couldn't hear it in her voice. Ruth had a quiet strength. She was one of those people who carried others' burdens and made the load a little lighter. At that moment, as they stood at the gate of the city Naomi dreaded, Ruth was all Naomi had to lean on. She knew that without Ruth she would have given up in the middle of the desert.

"That's it," Naomi answered.

Then Naomi saw someone she knew in the near distance. She tried to duck out of the way to avoid her gaze.

"What are you doing?" Ruth asked. "You're acting like a crazy person."

But it was too late. The woman had looked over and, to Naomi's surprise, instantly had recognized her.

"Naomi! Naomi! Hey, girl!"

Naomi now hated the sound of her name. To her, it served as a cruel reminder that life hadn't worked out as pleasantly as she'd hoped.

"Naomi! That you, girl? Where you been?" The woman came running over, waving her hands and causing a scene.

Soon other people in the city joined in. "Naomi's back, everybody! Let's party!"

In that moment, Naomi decided it was all too much.

The pain.

The lost dream.

She would break if she had to hear her name one more time.

"Please don't call me that," she said. "Call me Mara."

When she arrived back in her hometown, she knew she could no longer be known as pleasant. She chose a new name that better described her current circumstance and the sick feeling inside her stomach. She needed something to express how unfair life had been to her. So she went with the name Mara, which in Hebrew means "bitter."

This is what she wanted others to call her. This is how she felt.

Bitter.

THE TRAP

Naomi didn't realize what was going to happen next. Because she only saw her current circumstance and what she didn't have and how unfair life was, she couldn't see what tomorrow had in store for her.

She couldn't see that she would eventually help her daughter-in-law marry. She couldn't see that Ruth would bless her with a grandchild. And she couldn't see the amazing heritage that was before Ruth and her children. King David and Jesus Christ himself came from their family line! Yes, Jesus Christ, as in the savior of the world. I don't know about you, but I'd say that Naomi's life was kind of a big deal because of this. Because she couldn't see this coming, though, she wanted to be called Mara.

That's the thing about bitterness. It blinds you. It clouds your vision with the thoughts of everything you don't have and all the things that didn't work out, ultimately preventing you from seeing what could come next.

I like the way poet Maya Angelou described it. She said,

"Bitterness is like cancer. It eats upon the host."[1] Not only will bitterness hinder you from seeing what's coming next, but it also infects your whole life and those around you like a sickness.

Martin Luther King Jr., who had every reason in the world to carry bitterness around with him, said, "Never succumb to the temptation of becoming bitter."[2]

I don't believe in lost causes. When things don't work out as planned or tragedy hits, you're not forever doomed. There's no need to change your identity and wallow in your pain. As long as you have a pulse, you have a chance. Sometimes you have to wait for God to provide and come through for you, as he did for Naomi. If someone had told the poor widow when she lost everything that she would eventually have a grandchild, how would she have handled her situation differently? I'm sure she wouldn't have gone through the process of changing her name.

Similarly, if someone had walked up to Julia and me as we faked smiles during Thanksgiving insanity and told us about Winston, we might have responded differently. We might not have driven away with quite the same cancer-like bitterness infecting our bodies.

Let me tell you about Winston Charles, or as they call him on the streets, "Dub-C, my little gangster baby."

He is our healthy one-year-old boy who now brings so much joy to our lives. We are able to watch him take his first steps, say his first words, and drum on restaurant tables. We are able to celebrate his development while still loving on our Georgia. Before we had Winston, our home was very gloomy. Though we had faith for Georgia's healing, we found the reality that our only child was extremely sick difficult to face every day.

But then our little sunshine came along. With Winston, the burden of smooth brain became a little easier to bear. He's now too young to explain this to, but I look forward to one day telling him how he brought joy back into our lives.

Before he arrived, Julia and I found very quickly that bitterness was nothing more than a cruel trap. We discovered that if we sat and compared ourselves to other "normal" families—resentment brewing inside us about our circumstance—we got nowhere. Rather than moving forward and stepping into all that God has in store, we'd just be walking right into an impasse.

We needed the right perspective about what God promised. We had to cling to Job's words in the Bible. In Job 2, Job had a conversation with his wife after the devil himself put Job in a terrible physical situation.

So Satan went out from the presence of the LORD and afflicted Job with painful sores from the soles of his feet to the crown of his head. Then Job took a piece of broken pottery and scraped himself with it as he sat among the ashes.

His wife said to him, "Are you still maintaining your integrity? Curse God and die!"

He replied, "You are talking like a foolish woman. Shall we accept good from God, and not trouble?"

In all this, Job did not sin in what he said. (vv. 7–10)

Job's wife chose the bitterness route. To her, it was the natural response to something as terrible as death and sores. But Job didn't choose to throw in the towel or deem his life worthless to God. Rather, he chose not to sin and asked, "Can we accept only good things from God?"

If you don't know Job or haven't read his story, grab a box of tissues and prepare to get pretty depressed. Job's life wasn't fair, but he served as a beautiful example of how we are to handle things when it seems life has more downs than ups. Because this is how life is. Even life with God involves ugly sickness and death.

It's hard for some to accept that life with God isn't fairer than life without God. The same life our parents told us about when we'd get grounded and scream, "That's not fair!"

What was their reply? "Life's not fair."

We all experience a different dose of the unfair life. Trials of one kind or another are guaranteed to happen, and when they do, we'll all be tempted to let bitterness take its course or respond as Naomi and Job's wife did.

We could curse God, blame him for all our troubles, and let these troubles consume us and kill us. But I would encourage you in another direction. Don't let your mind fill with Job's wife's words. Don't "curse God and die." Live with integrity and discover a more abundant life.

The struggle is real. If we can't accept the bad and remove our blindfolds for tomorrow, we'll hit a dead end. That's not what Julia and I wanted for our family. That's not what we wanted for our Georgia.

The author of Hebrews put it perfectly: "Watch out that no poisonous root of bitterness grows up to trouble you, corrupting many" (12:15 NLT).

Having tasted bitterness, I know this to be true. You have to think of bitterness as a contagious disease that not only affects your life but also destroys those around you. It affects the way you treat others, the way you view the world, and the positive, exciting, vision-inspired decisions you make for your life.

Does this mean that pain should be ignored? Absolutely not.

There's a long list of things that Georgia can't do that her cousins can. There's a huge string of photos that will never be posted on social media, where Georgia looks special and her cousins do not.

And these things often hurt us so much that we get angry. But does that mean we should change our identities and forever be referred to as "Bitter"? Should we buy bumper stickers that read "We are the poor parents of a special-needs kid" or change our social media handles to

@sadchad and @sadjulia? Because things hurt and we're upset about them, do we want bitterness to become part of our identities? No way. We're not a depressing ad on TV asking people to donate to our cause for only thirty cents a day. We don't want to be a message of sorrow and pain. What would that add to the world? How would the beautiful message that comes from Jesus be reflected in that?

We knew we had an ugly sickness in our lives; it was time for us to look forward, away from our circumstance and toward the remedy.

In Conclusion . . .

You may be encountering a struggle of your own. It's possible that you read my story and find it all laughable. "Chad, you think *you* have problems? I'll show you problems," you might say.

As I've said before, it's not about comparisons. Over the course of our lives, we will all experience a struggle of one kind or another. We are not alone when we encounter heartbreak, death, or sickness. But when the worst of times comes, when we're forced to face these trials, our goal should not be to try to smile them away, to ignore the pain and suffering, or to shove them down into a deep, dark place.

So what should our goal be?

It's easy to panic in the midst of the storm as the disciples did in the boat—when, with blank minds, we forget who is by our side and assume the absolute worst. But panic cannot be our next step. In fact, panic often prevents us from taking any next steps at all.

It's also easy to let this trouble of ours fester and stew beneath the surface, resulting in anger and depression deep down below the feigned happiness. We find someone else to blame, whether God or doctors or others, and resent them throughout our day. If we let it, bitterness then easily infects and destroys our lives. It turns our tragic situations into something much worse, lives not lived to their fullest. Ignoring the greater plan God has at work, we wear bitterness like a weight that prevents us from moving forward or accomplishing anything.

Action Steps

What do we do, then? What actions or steps can we take when all seems lost and horrible? As I've said, nowhere in the Bible does God promise us a safe journey. Nowhere does it claim that there's a magic button he can push to take all our pain away and free us from our struggle. It doesn't tell stories about individuals who skip through life completely unharmed. That just isn't the way it works.

If you're searching for next steps amidst your storm, here are some practical ways you *can* cope with this reality:

1. Remember that God is with you. He will never leave or forsake you.

We have to remember that God is by our side. We know this from Jesus' last words in Matthew 28:20. "And surely I am with you always," he promises, "to the very end of the age." This statement reveals that Jesus is with us today, no matter what, fighting our battles with us. He's right by our side.

I know that he's willing to stand by me and comfort me while I cope with our family's circumstances, and he's willing to do the same for you. He won't leave you. He won't abandon you. To protect yourself and others, you must remember this important truth.

2. Praise God before the breakthrough. Praise him before the miracle appears.

This next step might seem strange. When trials hit, if God is going to enter the equation for you at all, your natural reaction is most likely not to worship him. You might turn to him with vulnerability, yell at him, lay your problems all out on the line, and generally vent your frustrations to him about your storm. I truly believe there's nothing wrong with this, but don't solely focus on the negative or let this frustration take up your entire time with God, especially if you have a relationship with him. As you remember the God by your side and all his amazing qualities—his love, his grace, and his power—thank him and praise him for them!

Follow the words of 1 Thessalonians 5:18: "In everything give thanks; for this is the will of God in Christ Jesus for you" (NKJV). Even before your miracle has occurred, you need to praise God. Don't wait until he's done something. Rather, praise him for who he is and who he'll always be. Many times when I've chosen to do this during my family's battle with Georgia's brain disorder, I've found the whole thing much easier to deal with. I find my perspective shifting. Bitterness and panic fade away when you praise and thank God for who he is even before your miracle comes.

3. Surround yourself with people who will speak life over you and your situation.

"Haters" always have something negative and awful to say. You know the ones. Often, they're easier to turn to when you want to sit in your horrible situation and don't really want a way out.

It's so crucial that you do not turn to these people in your hour of need. Instead, find the cheerleaders. Find the people who will speak words of hope, encouragement, and life when you need them most. Find the people that Proverbs 27:17 describes: "As iron sharpens iron, so one person sharpens another." Do you currently have someone sharpening you? Do you have people around you who like to dream big, who smile and laugh a lot, who always know exactly what to say? Is there someone by your side who tends to have more faith than others and says "You will" instead of "You'll never"?

I encourage you to take a serious look at your life. Think about all the relationships you have. What types of friends are these? Are you surrounding yourself with haters, or are you surrounding yourself with cheerleaders?

The community surrounding Julia and me has helped tremendously in our situation. We're fortunate to have many friends who encourage us, make us laugh, and bring us life. We can talk with these friends about Georgia and about the sorrow in our lives, and we always leave feeling better about the whole thing. They've been one of the most invaluable aspects of this journey. I'm not sure how we would survive without them.

Who's encouraging you?

4. Don't get bitter; get better.

Naomi let her situation define who she was. She decided she would be bitter, and because of this, she ruled out any other possibilities for her life. The truth is that trials, though horrible to endure, can often teach us a ton. We can learn from them and even come out of them as better human beings.

Whether gaining new empathy and compassion for others or learning to rely more and more on God, it is possible to come out of your situation stronger, healthier, and better. Bitterness will only prevent you from getting there.

5. Don't let the enemy convince you that you're the only one going through something.

The enemy likes to get into your thoughts when difficulties arise. He likes to whisper things like, "No one really understands what you are going through. You have it worse than everyone else."

Be wary of this trap. If you let yourself believe that you're the only one going through something, you'll lose the ability to have compassion and mercy for others. We're all going through our own struggles, pain, and difficulties. Let your situation only increase the empathy you feel for others. Don't let it isolate you.

6. Get perspective.

Again, this practical step involves not distancing yourself from others and not rehashing your situation over and over again alone. It's important to have a solid perspective of the trial that you're currently enduring. I've found two strategies that work when fighting to gain a healthy perspective of my circumstance.

The first is processing with other people. This is where vulnerability again plays a huge role. We're meant to endure trials together and in community. Each person has his own take on your situation, and the more you talk with others and listen to what they have to say, the more well-rounded your understanding of your circumstance will be.

The second is journaling. Writing down what I'm going through has helped me process and better understand my situation. If I write down my emotions and thoughts in dark moments, then I can step away and read them later, this time viewing them with slightly different eyes. It's amazing to read an entry from the day before when I thought the world was ending and discover that the next day I feel very differently and view my situation much more rationally.

7. Don't make any major life decisions until you calm down, drink some water, and get a good night's rest.

Rest is so essential. It's evident in Genesis that rest was even important to God, who chose to rest after he created the earth.

If you are someone who, when facing something bad or experiencing a conflict, immediately goes into problem-solving mode and searches for the solution, my advice to you is to slow down. Many times it's good in moments of trouble to begin solving problems right away, but sometimes when news is not life threatening, we shouldn't respond right away with an action plan. When we discover our daughter's brain isn't developing, or when we get hurt by someone else's words or find ourselves having an argument with our boss, we typically feel a range of very big, very real emotions. These emotions may include anything from anger to sorrow to frustration to panic to anxiety. When emotions are pumping through our systems at a hundred miles per hour, it is not the best time to make major life decisions.

It's important to stay calm in these moments. I know it seems silly, but when you experience trauma, it's the practical things that you tend to forget first. Sleep a full eight hours and then, when you've calmed down and gained a healthy perspective, you can make some rational choices.

These are the steps I've found to work best when I'm smack-dab in the middle of a trial. They have shifted my thinking, made waking up in the morning possible, and helped me look to the remedy, to God, with the right attitude and posture. I know that with God and with the people he's placed around me it is possible to survive something like Georgia's sickness and to thrive even in the midst of it.

It's possible for me, and it's possible for you.

Part 2

THE REMEDY

Somebody Feed Georgia

According to NINDS, the National Institute of Neurological Disorders and Stroke, "The prognosis for children with lissencephaly depends on the degree of brain malformation. Many will die before the age of 10 years. The cause of death is usually aspiration of food or fluids, respiratory disease, or severe seizures."[1]

What exactly does this mean for the Veach family? It means that seizures are not the only enemy. In fact, after speaking to many doctors and professionals about the disorder, we discovered that though they were violent, seizures weren't even our *worst* enemy.

Go figure. There was something even more nightmarish in store for us. The truth is, the most common cause of death for children with lissencephaly has to do with their breathing and swallowing muscles, not with abnormal electrical discharges in the brain.

It is most likely that Georgia will not die from her brain abusing her with a terrible convulsion in the middle of the night, but rather from an inability to swallow her food or from choking on some sort of foreign object in her airway.

This is what we are up against. But thankfully, as I mentioned before, my wife is superwoman. And a very determined superwoman, at that. Some might even call her stubborn, but I like to say that when it comes to Julia Veach, the motto "Where there's a will, there's a way" has proven true. This has been her approach to all aspects of life, including momhood.

It's a common thing to have some difficulty with breast-feeding. (Guys, am I really talking about breast-feeding in this book? Yeah, this is happening!) Many women have issues with it and resort to formula and bottle-feeding to keep their babies healthy. Women will hear things such as, "Do the very best you can, but if it doesn't work out, don't beat yourself up about it."

This, however, was not an option for Julia after Georgia was born. She resolved that she would be a master of breast-feeding. Georgia was going to eat and be healthy, whether she liked it or not. But from day one, this was anything but easy.

"Something's wrong with me!" Julia would yell from the bedroom. "I have a problem. She doesn't want to feed. My body is way out of whack. Women since the beginning of time have been doing this. Why is it not working for me?!"

Julia thought it was all her fault.

And my father thought it was mine.

When Georgia was born, we nicknamed her "Peanut" because she was the tiniest little thing. We brought her home at seven pounds and half an ounce. Not preemie-size, but definitely tiny to us as new parents. I remember believing she would fly out of my arms if I wasn't careful.

Once she was home, she only got tinier. Because of her issues with feeding, she lost weight by the day. We Googled everything about how to help maintain her weight. As I mentioned, Julia was determined. If the Internet told her to stand on her head for two hours while eating a whole loaf of bread, she'd be ready to do it. And our search did turn up some interesting advice. One suggestion included strawberry milkshakes. Julia did not have a problem with this one.

I was out at the store with my Milk-Making Shopping List

when my dad decided to begin his lecture. Here I am, thirty-something years old, about to receive a very stern talking-to by my father.

"Chad, we need to talk about your wife."

My first clue that the lecture was creeping up on us came from the "need to talk" and his referring to Julia as "my wife." If it was a serious matter for Dave Veach, the parties involved somehow lost their proper-noun privileges. I instantly guessed this lecture would have to do with my responsibilities as a father and a husband.

"It's your duty to take care of your wife and your child."

Yep, there it was.

"I don't think you're feeding your wife enough, son. If she were eating enough, there'd be enough milk for the baby. You need to feed your wife."

It all felt very prehistoric. Man get food. Man bring food to wife. Man force wife to eat food. Julia was a grown woman with a healthy appetite. I didn't have to tell her to eat. She wasn't on some crazy diet, starving herself to take off the baby weight. I mean, I was buying the woman strawberry milkshakes, for crying out loud!

"Dad, Julia's eating," I answered matter-of-factly.

My mom was no better. "Julia's too skinny," I'd hear over the phone or read in one of her daily texts that was a paragraph of baby/wife weight-gain advice.

I tried not to get upset at them or at Julia when she'd take the entire thing out on herself and slip into a deep depression. After all, everyone was simply worried about Georgia. Everyone wanted her to grow and thrive. I think it's easy to look for someone to blame when something isn't happening as expected. And so we blamed ourselves, and we blamed others.

At the start, it never entered our minds that Georgia wasn't eating because of some larger reason. We never assumed her swallowing muscles weren't working properly, never guessed she was having trouble developing that part of her body.

Ultimately Julia, in all her stubborn glory, managed to get Georgia to eat and gain some weight. Did Georgia eat perfectly? Did we defeat all the odds? Not exactly. There still remained a little bit of envy when we spent time with Julia's sister, who had a newborn of her own. Natalie made the whole breast-feeding thing seem so easy. We tried to be happy for her, but inside, I know it killed Julia. Her worst fear was that she wasn't a good enough mother, that something was wrong with her.

When we discovered lissencephaly and the doctors told us what the NINDS had to say, suddenly everything became clear.

It wasn't Julia; it was Georgia's disorder.

Thus began our search for the remedy. Some giant, worry-filled questions stretched across our parental brains: "How will we get Georgia to eat food? Will Georgia ever learn to eat? How do we keep our child from starving?"

Again, it all felt really prehistoric.

In our earliest visits to the doctor, two words were mentioned frequently. They felt very much like swear words.

"Eventually Georgia will need a feeding tube," they said. "We recommend she get it as soon as possible, especially if you have found issues with feeding."

Feeding tube.

It's hard to describe why in those early days a feeding tube sounded so repulsive to us. I suppose it's because at the time Georgia seemed pretty normal. Yes, she didn't keep her head up. Yes, she did have trouble keeping food down and tended to spit up. But when we got the diagnosis, she was a little more than four months old. This is the general point to which smooth brain kids will develop.

Up to that point, she looked and acted pretty much like a

three-month-old should. As you do with most three-month-olds, we held her, we bathed her, we changed her diapers, and we fed her. It was all very standard baby stuff.

A feeding tube, on the other hand, did *not* sound standard. It sounded ugly and, for some reason, felt like something you get only when you've given up. And remember, Julia Veach does not give up.

"Would you like to schedule the feeding tube in the next couple of months?" the doctor asked.

"No, we'll continue to feed her on our own," Julia answered. I waited for a "thank you, very much!" but it didn't come. I bet it was what she was thinking when she said it, though.

That wouldn't be the last time the doctors asked us this question, and it wouldn't be the last time Julia answered this way. Every time we went in they brought it up, dropped words like *recommend*, and showed us pamphlet after pamphlet.

And every time we politely refused.

You may be wondering why. *Why refuse a doctor's recommendation? Why say "no" so many times? Shouldn't you always heed the advice of the professionals? Were you trying to starve your child to death?*

I should probably explain that there was never a have-to involved in the whole scenario and that the doctor's recommendation always came with a caveat: "A feeding tube will decrease your daughter's ability to thrive."

For Georgia, a feeding tube would eventually decrease her muscle memory. Because she would get used to being fed through the tube, she would forget how to swallow with her mouth. We wanted to put this off as long as possible.

Truth was, though Georgia spat up often, she was still keeping a majority of her food down. She was still gaining weight. We knew that the tube would be inevitable, like a wheelchair of some kind would, but for the time being, we planned to wait until it was absolutely necessary.

After the MRI and the EEG and the diagnosis, the doctors recommended that we submit our three-month-old to yet another study. This time they wanted to study how Georgia swallowed. At the moment, they could only theorize how she was swallowing because of how lissencephaly kids tend to swallow. They wanted to know for certain.

So they took an X-ray of her throat while she ingested some food. The results were exactly as they'd anticipated. Georgia's brain wasn't telling her throat mechanism to swallow properly. This is often seen in stroke victims as well. They have to eat pureed food because their brains forget to tell their throats to swallow. The food can penetrate too deeply, and fluid and solids get backed up all the way to their vocal cords. This leads to aspiration pneumonia, a respiratory disease that kills many smooth-brain kids.

After this study, we were ordered to monitor Georgia's swallowing carefully, to not overload her with food, to feed her slowly, and to limit the breast-feeding because of how deeply she was swallowing. We took this advice.

To limit the breast-feeding and increase the calories, we decided to switch to baby food packets. But even with the packets, feeding was atrocious, especially in the Bellevue condo where we lived.

I think now would be a good time to dive into the horror that was the Bellevue condo. As I've mentioned, the start of our marriage took place in Puyallup, Washington, where I was on staff as the Generations pastor. Before we moved down to Los Angeles to start a church, Julia and I spent almost two years in Bellevue, Washington. While there, we were on staff at the City Church, an amazing community where some of our closest friends also pastored. When we moved up there, we found a great condo to live in that was right in the middle of the city.

The condo was beautiful with gigantic windows and a stunning view. From our place, we could see the entire city, and we were close to all our favorite restaurants and shopping. The amenities were spectacular. Our schedules weren't going to be as packed with the new job, and we were excited to enjoy the season of serving alongside our friends while living it up in the Seattle area. Sounds ideal, right? You're probably wondering where exactly the horror comes into play.

The horror, of course, came because of Georgia's disorder. The Bellevue condo was where Georgia decided to have some of her worst incidents. When Julia and I look back on that condo, we remember sleepless nights, never-ending seizure episodes, and the feedings. Oh, the feedings.

With our revelation from Georgia's swallow study and her newfound love for throwing up and spitting up anything and everything, feedings were no easy task. You'd think we'd just be able to pop in a food packet, let her suck on it for fifteen minutes, and call it good, right? Wrong.

The entire process took a couple of hours. I have distinct memories of watching my wife tirelessly putting food in Georgia's mouth bit by bit for what seemed like ages. She was careful not to put too much food in one bite, careful not to force anything if Georgia was flailing around or was not ready to eat. Breakfast, lunch, and dinner soon became our entire day.

Though the feeding-packet-slow-eating remedy seemed to be working, it was anything but practical. And the throwing up was getting worse.

To truly understand how dark the Bellevue condo days really were, you need to know what a hassle it could be to get from home to the car. The journey went something like this:

- Push the elevator button.
- Wait, and wait, and wait for an elevator to arrive.
- Cram into a packed elevator filled with Bellevue's finest . . .
- and their dogs.
- If there's only room for one normal-sized human and not enough room for one normal-sized human plus one larger-than-normal-sized stroller, wave the elevator on. You'll get the next one. Fingers crossed.
- Upon arriving downstairs, transfer elevators to go to the parking garage.
- In the parking garage, search for your car while thinking, *I swear I parked it here last time. I park it here every time. Or do I?*

You can imagine what a hassle it was to repeat this process all over again.

One Sunday while I was away on a trip, Julia experienced much more than a hassle. She had an all-out Bellevue condo catastrophe. I called her that day to check in, and the tone of Julia's voice signified that she'd had it with the condo-to-parking-garage-combined-with-Georgia's-feedings thing. She was overwhelmed and sick of the throwing up.

She described to me the events of her morning. She had finished her hour-and-a-half feeding session, having woken up early enough to feed Georgia and get herself ready for church on time. Then she had put Georgia in one of her adorable outfits. Our girl was head-to-toe in that G-flow. She was wearing her Sunday best.

Then it was time to head out the door. Julia waited for the elevator, crammed inside, made the switch, and headed to the parking lot. When she got to the car, *bam!* Georgia decided it was the perfect time to throw up all over everything.

Not a big deal, Julia thought. *I can handle this. We might be thirty minutes late for church, but I'll just sneak in the back.*

So she headed up the elevators and back to the condo. Good thing G had plenty of outfits. Julia grabbed another, new shoes, new tights, new dress, new headband, and all. Somehow the throw-up had managed to get on everything. She cleaned Georgia up and headed down the stairs for round two.

Elevator 1.

Elevator 2.

Parking garage.

And . . .

Projectile vomit spewed out of Georgia again, leaving nothing unsoiled. Even Julia was covered in the fruit packet Georgia had consumed earlier that morning.

By this time, Julia was almost yelling as she retold the story to me on the phone. I knew she didn't actually blame my daughter for any of this, but sometimes you have to get mad at this whole smooth-brain thing. I mean, it's killing kids. Somebody's got to get mad!

"I'm so sorry," I said on the phone. "That sounds *awful.* I can't believe she did that twice in a row all the way down in the garage."

"Oh, no, no. Twice would've been fine. Twice would've been easy," Julia replied. Then she proceeded to tell me about the third and final time.

Julia decided that perhaps the third time would be a charm. At this point, she was about an hour late for service. Maybe, if she was lucky, she'd be able to catch the last five minutes of the sermon and a worship song. At least she'd get to socialize with people in the lobby. She'd begun to feel like she was seeing less and less of adult humans lately.

So she journeyed back up the elevator once more. This time she changed her own outfit, too, and opted for something a little less complicated for Georgia. Maybe no bow this time. With some new tights and Georgia's third-cutest dress, the two were off again for round three.

I don't know what it was about the parking garage at the Bellevue condo that made Georgia so gag-ready, but she obviously thought this was the best place to have her episodes. She couldn't do it right outside the condo. She couldn't get it out before they ever entered the elevator. That might have lost Julia only a few minutes, maybe. But this was not Georgia's style. She waited until the absolute last moment possible. It seemed she was waiting for the instant when Julia thought she was in the clear, believing they would soon be driving away to church, clean mommy and baby.

During the final attempt, Julia was extra careful as she lifted Georgia out of her stroller. At that point, she no longer cared about whether they actually got to the church building. It was Julia versus the throw-up, and she was going to be victorious. This final time, perhaps because of the special care she took lifting her into the car seat, Georgia made it to the buckle-up phase.

Julia strapped her in, sat down in the front seat, turned on the ignition, and Georgia seized her opportunity. Throw-up was everywhere . . . again. This time, it was all over the car.

Julia lost the game. Church was not in the cards for them that morning. Six elevator trips, three changes of outfits, and three baths later, Julia felt defeated. As she told me this on the phone, I was hit yet again by the fact that our girl was *sick*. I realized how much this disorder was affecting our lifestyle. I wanted to scream, get mad, or hit something. I knew God wouldn't be upset with me if I did all this, so I turned to him.

"Enough," I prayed that night, feeling helpless, worrying about my wife staying at home again for an entire day to scrub throw-up out of clothes. "God, we *cannot* live this way." I had a new resolve about the whole scenario. I felt as though God wasn't afraid of my "enoughs," wasn't scared by my desire to be rescued. "This is entirely overwhelming for our home. It leaks into everything. We can't do this anymore. We need a way out."

We needed the medicine, the antidote, and an absolute solution to our aspirating woes. When I arrived back home a couple of days later, I decided to bring up the topic to Julia. It was time to discuss the elephant in the room. It was time to talk *feeding tube.*

"Not yet," Julia answered.

She was still determined. The same woman who believed she could beat all odds and breast-feed her newborn was standing in my living room doing throw-up laundry. She was no quitter. She explained to me that Georgia had done better that day, that she was learning the right way to move Georgia and the right pace to feed her so that the throw-up was reduced.

Her eyes looked so tired. I could see the lack of sleep, the worry, and the physical exhaustion that came with carrying our growing toddler from the bathtub to the couch and back to the tub again. But behind this weariness was that constant strength. She was still the sassy woman I married, and I trusted her.

"Okay," I answered.

Julia came up with her own solution for avoiding apartment-to-car fiascos in the days following. Basically we would wrap Georgia in a million spit-up rags and blankets, meticulously covering every corner of her perfect outfit. Our daughter looked like a mummy. We gave awkward smiles and nothing-to-see-here glances to our neighbors who stared at us in the elevator. The mummy outfit would stay on from the apartment to the car and up until the very last possible moment. We'd pull up to the church and quickly whip it off of her; then we'd carry our baby in, looking clean and normal.

But the mummy wrap was only a temporary solution to an

ever-growing problem. And this problem wasn't our only one. We also had seizures to deal with. Remember those?

When you're attempting to feed the unfeedable, throw in some seizures for a rip-roaring good time. It was when her seizures got worse that feeding Georgia became downright impossible. There was really no time between seizures to feed her because she was having them up to fifty times a day.

It was when Georgia had gone a complete day without eating any food at all that Julia looked at me and said, "It's time." We admitted defeat. We could no longer feed Georgia on our own. The feeding tube we had dreaded was now truly necessary for our daughter's survival.

We called the doctor, hoping to book the procedure for the following day and get our quick-fix solution, but we were shocked to discover it wasn't quite that easy. There was a waiting period.

Looking back, it probably was not the wisest choice to wait until we were absolutely desperate to book the procedure. The few weeks we had to wait felt like years. Georgia had multiple days of not keeping down an ounce of food. She was getting skinnier and skinnier.

By the time we carried her down the elevators and loaded her into the car to head to Seattle Children's Hospital, she was so tiny, and we were so ready.

We were ready for relief from our struggle and ready to turn to someone else for a solution. We were ready for our remedy.

Yes, the feeding tube would be our savior and would eventually help Georgia eat again, but the throwing up didn't go away; it only lessened a bit. And that was the thing about lissencephaly: there seemed to be no true cure for it. There was no medicine to make it all go away. The seizure medication took away the seizures but also took away Georgia's personality. The feeding tube helped her eat, but the throwing up continued.

Things got better, yes. But there was no perfect remedy for the disorder, except for one, of course. There was one source that always offered a solution, the means of surviving it all.

That source was God.

Chapter Four

EVER-PRESENT HELP

It wasn't real. Couldn't be real. I felt as though I'd soon wake up and realize that I'd had a sick, demented dream.

The screams I had seen on the television, the chaos, the dust, the smoke, the explosion, the businessmen jumping from buildings . . . it all played in my head on a loop. No matter how hard I tried to change my mind's subject, I kept returning to what I'd watched.

It wasn't a movie. It wasn't a story of fiction. New York had been attacked.

And I, like so many others on the West Coast, was just a bystander. There was nothing I could do on that day as so many in New York suffered. I felt helpless. As did my other classmates.

We slowly walked into the chapel of our Bible college that Tuesday morning as we always did on Tuesdays. But this morning was much different. No one said anything. We shuffled slowly in and took our seats. The room was pretty much silent.

What could our professor say that would do any good? How would he respond to this evil? Perhaps he'd have some wise speech prepared that would make us feel better. But we all doubted it. No one had the right thing to say at that moment. We waited, patiently sitting in silence, haunted by the images we had seen.

Dr. Larry Powers walked up to the chapel pulpit with no introduction. Rather than rehashing the attacks in front of the crowd and discussing what had happened, he slowly opened a book. Rather than introducing a flashy sermon, he simply began to read: "God is our refuge and strength, an ever-present help in trouble."

As a Bible-college student and pastor's kid, I had heard Psalm 46 read aloud many times before. But this particular reading struck a different chord inside of me.

"Therefore we will not fear, though the earth give way and the mountains fall into the heart of the sea."

Suddenly I knew how to picture those words: *the earth give way.* I saw the businessman falling again. I saw the building exploding and the city filling with dust, and my professor picked up his cadence . . .

". . . though its waters roar and foam and the mountains quake with their surging."

His words boomed in the quiet auditorium as he read all 195 words of the passage to his captive audience.

"He says, 'Be still, and know that I am God'" (Ps. 46:1–3, 10).

And that's what we were.

Still.

WANNABE SUPERHEROES

When trouble hits, he'll be there.

When you think there's nowhere to turn, there he is.

When you cry for help from the abandoned streets, who shows up but . . .

Phoenix Jones Guardian.

Before you ask, "Who dat?" let me tell you a little story about a strange subculture of Seattle, Washington. This subculture consists of a band of costume-wearing vigilantes. That's right, we're talking real, live, wannabe superheroes.

In 2010, this group of ridiculous crime fighters roamed the streets of Seattle in search of damsels in distress. With genuine hearts to stop evil and genuinely terrible costumes, Thunder 88, Catastrophe, Knight Owl, and Captain Ozone (not making these names up) tried to save citizens from drug dealers, domestic abuse, robbery, and other terrible acts of injustice. They were out to clean the scum off the streets, save the innocent, defend the weak, and help the needy.

It was even reported in a Seattle newspaper that poor Phoenix Jones, the Guardian of the Emerald City (as he liked to call himself), was stabbed when trying to stop a criminal on the streets.

It was noble!

It was valiant!

It was stretchy-panted!

But was it asked for?

Like any good superheroes, these people had great intentions and really wanted to care for their city. But here's the thing: no one was crying for their help. In fact, most citizens were downright confused by the people roaming the streets in masks.

After all, in the real world, if we see a strange group of people walking around in costumes, most of us do not feel safer. In fact, we feel quite the opposite. It was reported that the citizens they were eagerly trying to save were locking themselves in their cars. Many were afraid that the strange, masked characters walking into local gas stations and shopping malls were going to rob the establishments or do something even worse.

I'm not sure exactly what response these "heroes" expected, but no one was dialing up the local authorities to say, "Turn on the Captain Ozone signal! We need him and *now!*"

No. Because unlike most superheroes we've seen flying across the screens in movie theaters, these vigilantes were real, common people. Real people who didn't care if someone was asking for their help, because, by golly, they were going to be there . . . with masks . . . whether the people liked it or not!

It's funny, but this whole strange happening reminds me a lot of

God. Before you wonder why a mask-wearing lunatic named Knight Owl reminds me of God, hear me out.

God doesn't wait for us to ask for help. He steps up when there's trouble. He walks in. He rises to the occasion.

Even though we often panic like Peter in the storm, he's right there whether we want him or not. And usually we do want him there. Because unlike a creepy guy roaming the streets with a strange alias, God is the perfect remedy to our struggle.

Lion's Lunch

I'd like you to read about one of the more famous stories of the Bible. It may not be told as often as the Christmas story or the moment David killed Goliath, but this story is up there and probably a part of the Top Ten Bible Stories Sunday School Teachers Like to Tell Children.

Ladies and gentlemen, I give you . . . Daniel and the Lion's Den.

If you grew up in the church, you can almost see the felt board now, can't you? You can visualize a kneeling, illustrated Daniel, staring up at heaven with a calm look on his face. You can see a couple of adorable little lions curled up in a sleeping position. It's all so cute and cuddly. Not.

Daniel and the Lion's Den is a tragic story. One that involves broken friendship, betrayal, and religious persecution. It's also a powerful story that reveals God's ability to pull us out of anything. Even the darkest pit.

When I read the story, I imagine Daniel being lowered into a cold, dark cave, thinking to himself, *What exactly have I gotten myself into?*

I'm sure he could hear them, a quiet rumbling in the corner—the lions. *This is going to be fun. Yep, I was really hoping to get ripped apart by lions today,* Daniel probably thought as his heart beat faster and faster. (The Daniel I imagine uses sarcasm as a coping mechanism.)

The poor guy was about to face off with nature's most vicious beast! Where were Val Kilmer and the rest of the cast of *The Ghost and the Darkness* when Daniel needed them?

When he landed in the pit, he probably searched around to count how many lions he had to deal with. *Is that three sets of eyes over there by that dark creepy shadow? Or four? Oh, no . . . it's six. Yep, six. Perfect.* (There goes that internal sarcasm again.)

Perhaps worse than the terrible situation itself was the reason why he was in it. It wasn't some distant tyrannical government that had put him in this pit. It wasn't some evil power he'd never met. It was his friend. He had been close friends with the king and had become a sort of confidant for him. Did they agree on everything? No. But still, Daniel considered him a good friend, and this entire situation was a betrayal.

The king's signature had made this terrible moment possible. He had signed the paper into law saying whoever prayed to Daniel's God would be torn apart by lions.

Daniel looked up at him from inside the cold cave. The king's eyes were filled with pain, almost as if to say, "This hurts me more than it hurts you."

Not likely, thought Daniel.

"I'm so sorry!" the king yelled down to the poor man in the dark cave next to the pack of lions.

That's great! Daniel thought. *So how about you just undo it, huh? After all, you're the one who made the law in the first place! The one who decreed that praying to God meant death by lion. Maybe you could, you know . . . make a new law or something?*

But Daniel knew things didn't work that way, so he kept his mouth shut. His friend, the king, simply couldn't undo something like this. Thinking like that would only be futile.

Instead, Daniel focused his thoughts elsewhere. He had more important things to worry about now. Like surviving and lion-dodging. He thought back to the moment that had gotten him into this situation.

He recalled how praying to the God he loved and worshiped in his own home had led him to this cave. Somehow, knowing this gave him peace. *If that's what leads to my death,* Daniel thought with confidence, *then so be it.*

The ceiling began to shake as a giant stone was rolled across the entrance of the cave. His "friend" was now gone. Everything was black. The little peace Daniel had mustered started to fade.

I don't know about you, but if I were Daniel, I would have freaked out right around this moment. Dark cave—bad. Hungry lions—bad. No way out—really bad.

Daniel's freak-out most likely began when the cave door closed. I'm sure he turned to every corner of that dark cave, breathing heavily. Were the lions to the right? To the left? Was there any way out? Perhaps his friend had made some sort of escape for him?

Bam! I imagine him running right into a giant lump on the ground as he searched the cave for hope. The lump felt kind of like a fuzzy kitten, but this cat was big enough to kill a grown man.

It probably weighed twice as much as Daniel, and its teeth were sharper than knives. He gulped and clenched his fists, waiting for the beast to attack.

All right, kitty kitty. Give me your best shot. Dear God, help me.

But nothing happened.

Daniel's muscles loosened as he realized the lion was sleeping. They were *all* sleeping! He heard their heavy breaths and the sound of purring. The young man began to laugh as he realized the absurdity of the situation. He was a fresh snack, but the lions were sleeping through the whole thing!

He knew who had caused these animals to sleep, who had saved him—his helper, his God.

The book of Daniel says:

Then the king returned to his palace and spent the night without eating and without any entertainment being brought to him. And he could not sleep.

At the first light of dawn, the king got up and hurried to the lions' den. When he came near the den, he called to Daniel in an anguished voice, "Daniel, servant of the living God, has your God, whom you serve continually, been able to rescue you from the lions?"

Daniel answered, "May the king live forever! My God sent his angel, and he shut the mouths of the lions. They have not hurt me, because I was found innocent in his sight. Nor have I ever done any wrong before you, Your Majesty." (Dan. 6:18–22)

The lions were sitting there, quiet and still. "God sent his angel." God "shut the mouths of the lions." God rescued Daniel.

FEEDING TUBE TO THE RESCUE

Please, someone rescue me from this place, I thought as I sat still, staring at the clock.

The hospital room smelled the way all hospital rooms smell—like hand sanitizer and bad cafeteria food. I could hear kids in the rooms down the hallway, some crying, some yelling, others laughing. We knew that other desperate parents were waiting around in those rooms. We were right there with them, waiting for Georgia to be taken out of surgery.

Have we really already been here for ten hours? I thought.

I had imagined the scenario going down differently. We'd be greeted by a smiling doctor. "Hello, there!" he'd say with a wave. "Here's your feeding tube!" Just like that, he'd pop the feeding tube device into G's tummy, hand us an instruction manual titled "The Feeding Tube and You" (complete with illustrations), pat our backs, and send us on our way. Then our aspiration, two-hour feedings, constant throwing up, three trips up and down the elevator problems would be solved!

That is not exactly what happened.

We had to stay at the hospital for two days while the feeding tube was inserted and Georgia recovered from the surgery. The whole thing was a bit overwhelming. That first day consisted of listening to doctor after doctor, sitting, waiting, and praying in between breaths. But throughout the day, I remembered the commitment Julia and I had made at the start of our journey.

Before we had a sick kid of our own, we had seen other parents with similar issues posting online. Their paragraphs-long posts basically exclaimed "Woe is me!" with details of every problem they faced. They were being real, yes. Desperate times call for desperate measures, true. But something was missing from their posts. Amid all the terrible news, they ignored the "ever-present help in trouble," the God who was right there with them. Everything was the worst, and they failed to acknowledge what the Best had in store for them.

Shortly after the diagnosis, Julia and I committed to having a "positive confession." We wanted to declare good things about the whole situation and not bad. When things got terrible, we wanted to look for something good to thank God for despite it all. If Georgia was having difficulty eating, we were going to celebrate the times she was able to keep food down! If we felt that terrible urge to compare coming over us again, we would celebrate our daughter, the lessons God was teaching us, and the beautiful family he had created for us.

When we made that commitment a year prior to Georgia's surgery, we didn't know how difficult this task would be.

As I sat there in the hospital room, I tried to shift my perspective from "sad dad who spends weekend in hospital" to "God's child who has someone by his side." Immediately, I started viewing my environment differently.

I looked at the nurses with a different set of eyes. They were so attentive to Georgia and ready to help us when necessary. They were a gift to our family. I was suddenly amazed at the wealth of knowledge the doctors had about Georgia's illness. They knew exactly what our daughter needed, because they had worked with other kids like her and had devoted years to studying and understanding disorders like hers. Finally, I realized that the feeding tube itself was a miracle.

I was in awe that God had gifted someone with enough imagination and brainpower to invent a device to feed those who have no way of feeding themselves. This wonderful tube was going to help my daughter.

The more I searched for my ever-present God, the more I found that he was just that—*everywhere*. On my day of trouble, he stepped in.

As I took in my surroundings, I decided I, too, would post on social media. I snapped a picture of our girl in her hospital bed and wrote simply, "Thanks so much, Seattle Children's. Successful surgery." And that's when God, our superhero, showed up yet again.

My phone began to buzz like crazy. Likes, tags, at-mentions, texts, tweets, and *love* spilled through social media. Diagnosis day and our announcement seemed so long ago now, after so many months of feeling as though we were facing this monster alone.

But that one post again revealed the community we had surrounding us. God showed himself to us through *people*. The support was more than we could have ever anticipated or expected. It gave us new peace and joy.

ALL AROUND

The day of trouble.

This is God's specialty. This is the day God reveals how helpful and powerful he is. On September 11, he provided community for families who faced unbearable loss, and he gave hope to the hopeless. For Daniel he silenced the lions and put them into a peaceful sleep. For Julia and me he created a feeding tube so our daughter could eat without gagging and survive another day. He continually provides community and the love and support of others. He repeatedly reveals to us that we are not alone in this. And he uses situations to teach us about his character and the amazing God he is. What has he done for you? What is he currently doing for you?

Whether through people, miracles, or medicine, God wants to help—even loves to help—in the day of trouble. As he proves throughout the Bible, this is where he thrives. He draws near to comfort, defend, protect, and fight for you in the moment you need him most.

Imagine a situation that's desperately bad. Let's say you've found yourself in a yelling match with your spouse. Because of this argument, you feel alone and misunderstood. How will you ever resolve this? You want to leave, escape, or drive somewhere else, because staying put seems absolutely hopeless.

Then you hear a knock at the door. To your surprise, on the other side is a superhero. This is not a creepy superhero from Seattle wearing a DIY cape and going by the name of Marriage Problem-Solving Man. Visualize a superhero who can do all things and has the power to help with any situation. He knows what you and your spouse need to hear. He knows the right way to comfort you. On top of this, he knows you, your specific personality, your needs, your hopes and dreams. He's known you since you were born; even before that! When you realize he's there, the need to escape, the feeling that your circumstance will crush you, instantly vanishes and is replaced by peace and a belief that something better is in store for your tomorrow.

That's the God I know.

And the wonderful thing about him? He's always at the front door. There's no waiting period with this superhero. You don't have to shine a sign into the sky and wait for him to fly over to your house. He's there, and he's all around.

Some people have a hard time grasping this. They think God is absent when they're facing their dark circumstances or that he has somehow abandoned them and left them to face things all alone. "That's easy for you to say, Chad. But where's God in *my* situation, huh?" "Why would a good God let something like this happen? I don't see God anywhere in this."

You may feel this way because you've yet to know God and understand him. To you he is distant and maybe sometimes even cruel. I believe many people feel this way about God because they're not looking for him.

When you look for God, you'll find him all around you.

Searching for God is like the easiest game of Where's Waldo. Once you start realizing how he's provided something for you or the people he's placed in your life, you'll see him everywhere you turn. He'll be less and less difficult to spot, and as you realize this, you'll find it easier and easier to face your problems.

That fight you had with your spouse will seem so small compared to the big things God has done for you. The job you lost last week and the accompanying feeling of failure will be replaced by new opportunities and visions for the future. A daughter who has a rare brain disorder will reveal to you how much of a comforter and father God can be when you need him most.

After our two-day visit and hours of waiting, the Veach family finally left the hospital with a brand-spanking-new feeding tube. Because we had looked for God at the hospital and saw all that he was providing for us, we also left with a clearer understanding of the true remedy for our struggle.

We'd soon need to rely on this remedy more and more as we realized the tube came with its own set of unique, "exciting" challenges. It seemed there was always something new for us to learn.

Operation "Fatten Up Georgia" had begun, and though, as Psalm 46 says, the waters seemed to roar around us and the mountains seemed to quake, we were learning every day to be still and know that God was right there with us. We clung to promises like these:

"Many are the afflictions of the righteous, but the LORD delivers him out of them all" (Ps. 34:19 NKJV).

"We are hard pressed on every side, but not crushed; perplexed, but not in despair; persecuted, but not abandoned; struck down, but not destroyed" (2 Cor. 4:8–9).

"And we know that in all things God works for the good of those who love him, who have been called according to his purpose" (Rom. 8:28).

He is exactly what we need to get through this life. We can get through any circumstance with him by our side.

Chapter Five

THERE'S ALWAYS
MORE WITH GOD

LET ME TELL YOU ABOUT AN INTERESTING BREED OF PEOPLE. They're living among us. You'll find them at your workplace, in your circle of friends, and maybe even in your own families. These people are not normal. They enjoy inflicting pain on themselves, adhering to strange diets, and on any given day, they might be flipping around giant tires for the "fun" of it.

CrossFit people.

How do you know one of these weirdos is among you? Just check your Facebook feed. They've probably posted about their box jumps three times in the last hour, because CrossFit is the opposite of Fight Club. The first rule of CrossFit is you always talk about CrossFit.

Phil Dooley, a friend of mine and the lead pastor of Hillsong South Africa, is one of these people. When I visited his church in 2014, he placed me in a socially awkward position. He introduced me to eleven dudes from his "box," another strange CrossFit practice I won't pretend to understand . . . like wearing Reeboks.

Have you ever met someone and immediately known there is no hope for a friendship? Have you ever instantly realized that there's no way longevity will be in the cards for your new relationship? Have you ever been in a position where interaction with a particular human being feels strictly obligatory? Every now and then, I find myself in this place, smiling through it, hoping for the best and waiting for it to pass as all things do.

Welcome to Chad Meets Eleven Giant CrossFit Dudes.

"Hi, I'm Chad."

"NICE TO MEET YOU, PUNY MAN WITH SKINNY LEGS," the eleven men seemed to yell as they towered over me.

Well, that wasn't so bad, I thought. *I'll go back to my day now.* I gave a small wave and tried to turn around. However, Phil Dooley decided to trap me.

"You know, guys, Chad's flight doesn't leave until tomorrow night. Don't you think he should work out with us?"

Phil was suddenly the worst type of friend to have. He saw the painstaking conversation I'd had with these giant men; he had sensed the incompatibility. He knew how terrible I would look at a gym next to them, yet he forced me into answering that inevitable question.

"So, Chad, what do you say? Pick you up in the morning?" I was ready to smack the grin right off of Phil's face. Somehow, I managed to force out a "yes."

Remorse immediately followed.

That night in my hotel room, I found myself pacing. *What have I done? How am I going to do this? What am I going to wear? Will they accept me if I show up in Nikes?*

This got me nowhere, so I switched gears into pump-up mode. *You are a thirty-five-year-old man.* I looked at myself in the mirror. *You have kids. You have a mortgage payment and four chest hairs. You can do this!*

The next morning I walked in with my head held high. I stood with the giant men and listened as the cult leader, Al, gave us instructions.

"Here's what we're gonna do!" he yelled through his manly beard. "We're gonna do box jumps. We're gonna do burpees. We're gonna run outside in the cold. We're gonna come back in here, and we're gonna do wall squats."

I got this, I thought. And the workout began.

I am not exaggerating when I tell you, I really did have it. I crushed that workout. I killed the box jumps, I aced the burpees, and I ran outside like a boss. When the wall squats arrived, I used the adrenaline I'd pumped up throughout the other exercises and totally nailed them.

Now, before I tell you what I did next, I'd like to describe the type of person I am. I love being affirmed after I've done something well. I'm the guy who puts one dish in the dishwasher at home and looks around to see if anyone noticed. "Did you see that? I put the dish in!" I will shout through the house. I imagine my wife will hear this and race to the kitchen, her eyes filled with happy tears, to proclaim how amazing I truly am.

"My hero! He put away a dish! Oh, how did I ever get so lucky to find such a man?"

When it comes to a good workout, I'm no different. When my wall squats were done, I jumped up and started looking around the room for someone to affirm me.

But no affirmation came that day. No "Wow, Chad! You're really awesome! I can't believe you did it!" from my buddy Phil. No praise at all from the large men when they saw me holding my ground during CrossFit. No one seemed to care that I did an exceptional job, and I quickly understood why.

Al stood in front of the group with a stoic expression and said, "All right, guys. Great warm-up. Now it's time for the real workout."

More is not always a good thing.

That is, unless you're talking about God. The longer I live the more I find that this is true. He *always* has more for us. And not in the more-painful-workout kind of way (though he does dish out some of that as well). He has more for us in the bonus-track-on-your-2002-CD, secret-scene-at-the-end-of-the-movie-theater-credits kind of way.

You haven't even seen his best card yet because he reveals himself in increments. Every day, there's more of him for you to discover and more for you to receive. And when it comes to God, more is good no matter how you look at it. He provides, he comforts, he teaches, and he goes above and beyond what you could ever expect. I will definitely pass on more CrossFit and, to prevent a Reebok fetish or unnecessary injury, encourage you to do the same. But I will never pass on the more God has for me.

When More Is Good

That's it. No more just sitting, listening to cute sermons, or singing good songs. It's time to tell him my real issues and see how he responds.

These were the woman's thoughts as she pounded on the door. It had taken a lot for her to head to her pastor's house. It was easy to assume he had more important things to do than to hear her problems, but she was at her breaking point.

The day before she had spent her last cent. She had no job opportunities, and worst of all, they were going to take her sons.

She pounded again.

He had to leave me with all of this debt, didn't he? she thought of her husband, who had recently passed away. The collectors were a-knockin', which meant if she didn't have the funds to repay them, her sons would become their property. They would become slaves, have to serve unpaid.

She went to knock a third time, but the door swung open.

Her pastor, Elisha, was standing there. Before he could say anything, she blurted it all out. She talked about her husband, she talked about all the money she owed, she talked about her sons. Things had gotten real. She waited for Elisha to pass her off to someone else or say a prayer and send her on her way, but she wasn't going to take no for an answer. She needed help *now*.

"What do I do?!" she yelled.

Elisha, cool, calm, and collected, responded, "Well, what do you have in your house?"

Ha! she thought. *This'll be good. Now he'll really know how impossible my problem is.*

"What do you have?" he asked again.

"I have one jar of . . . *oil.*"

She waited for the laugh. But Elisha thought for a moment, then looked her in the eyes. "Go ask your neighbors for some empty jars they're not using. Once you've collected them, go home, shut the door, and pour the oil you have into the empty jars."

The plan sounded absolutely absurd, but the woman was desperate. She'd give anything a chance right now, even if it meant lugging a bunch of empty jars to Elisha's house at three in the morning, pounding on the door, and showing him how she still had only one small jar of oil to her name.

She did as he said. Soon her house was filled with empty jars, one from each of her obliging neighbors. She shut the doors.

The empty vessels that lined her kitchen seemed like a joke now. *Maybe that's what Elisha meant all along,* she thought. *Maybe this is all to serve as a terrible metaphor of how empty my life is. No husband. No money. I'm like an old, empty jar.*

She shook off this feeling and did just as he said. *Here goes nothing . . .*

She and her sons began pouring the small jar of oil into one of the empty jars. To her surprise, the first one filled right up. It was the largest jar of the group! *There's no way this is possible,* she thought, then eagerly grabbed another jar. That one filled up as well; so did the next and the next, until each and every jar in her house was filled.

God had given her enough oil to pay off her debts and save her sons! She had much, much more than when she started.

When I imagine this story from 2 Kings 4, I always place myself in the woman's shoes. How many times have I felt similarly, as though I had so little of value to my name? And yet, this little that I have is exactly what God can use to bless me.

WHEN DISNEY HURTS

Having a "God has more for me" attitude is often easier said than done. Since Georgia's disorder came into our lives, all too often Julia and I find ourselves responding negatively to trials. Rather than face each day with a "we got this" attitude, sometimes we forget our best behavior. Sometimes our pain manifests itself in anger, frustration, and marital disputes. When we don't express how hard this situation really is and don't come clean with our fears and sorrows, these emotions can boil up and erupt in an ugly fashion. This is what happened on Disney Day.

On that morning, our house was a whirlwind.

We had just moved to LA, and the first visitors to our new home were the in-laws. Julia's mom, two of her sisters, their husbands, and three little kids were in town for the weekend. The house was packed. Suitcases were everywhere, along with bodies sleeping on the couch, sleeping on the floor, making up camp for the weekend. There was laughter, there was chaos, there were tears, and what pairs well with all of these? Why, a day at Disneyland, of course!

Sometimes when you're traveling with a crew of thirteen, it's not so much the Disneyland experience itself that's stressful as much as getting out the door. For us, the moments leading up to the happiest place on earth were anything but happy.

Our little nephews, Scout and Wallace, had no idea the surprise that was in store for them. It was all planned. We would drive down to that magical place, and right when we pulled up to the doors, we would tell them, "We're going to Disneyland!" Pull out your iPhones, snap a photo, get a video, because magic is a'comin'.

Those little faces flashed through our minds when we woke up that Monday morning. But as Julia and I lay in our bed, slowly getting up to face the day, we found ourselves not feeling very excited. We could hear our son screaming from his crib. Suddenly, the anticipation that had been building up all weekend lost its glamor. The idea of Disneyland strangely didn't seem all that great. This was perhaps because we realized Scout and Wallace were in for the surprise of their lives, and we were wondering to ourselves, *What is Georgia in for?*

I lay there, imagining Disney Day being like any other day for her. She would only lie in her stroller, staring into space, unaffected by the magic.

Comparison was rearing its ugly head once again.

I wish I could tell you that I woke up that morning with a different feeling. I wish I could say I tried to think about how much more God had in store for us that day. If only I could tell you that we put on smiles and Mickey shirts and skipped out the door.

What really happened was World War III.

I didn't realize it at the time, but Julia woke up with similar visions flashing through her mind. And the icky feeling that had greeted us before our morning coffee soon leaked into everything else.

"What do you think you're doing?"

"Hello! Can I get some help?"

There was yelling.

There were ugly words.

Over the course of an hour, we somehow found a million things to fight about. This included whose turn it was to feed Georgia, why one of us got to drink coffee while the other wrestled to get clothes on Winston, why one of us reacted with an unacceptable look, why the Lakers were so bad, and more. Doors slammed and kids screamed. And all the while, there were still in-laws, watching quietly, trying not to get caught in the cross fire.

In the moments leading up to Disneyland, I found myself so

upset about the morning routine and the way Julia was handling everything in front of her family. My blood was boiling.

How could Julia get mad about a little thing like this? I thought. *So I drank coffee! What is the big deal? Why is she so frustrated and angry with me for everything? She's not even trying to have a good attitude.*

I thought I was only upset because of the way she had talked to me. I was already rehashing the things she said as we stormed out the door. My brain recounted the terrible accusations. I knew that if it came to a court case, I would have the winning argument. Or at least that's what I had convinced myself of.

But the truth was I was frustrated too. I was as upset as she was. And why? All the thoughts that circled my head only hid what I really needed to deal with.

I, too, was in the wrong. I, too, was upset about Julia, our crazy packed house, and the events of the morning. But I was lying to myself. I wanted to reassure myself that these events were all that had me bothered.

That was until I remembered the images that flashed through my brain that morning. Georgia in a stroller, unable to ride rides or take in the attractions. As we drove to Anaheim, it was clear that much more was going on underneath the surface for both of us. Halfway between LA and Anaheim, Julia began to cry.

"What's the point of bringing her to Disneyland if she can't enjoy it?" she said through sobs. "We should turn around and go home. Putting her in Mickey ears, dressing her up . . . why? She won't remember any of this."

Like the woman in 2 Kings whom Elisha sent out to gather empty jars, it seemed as though we were doing something pointless. But God had something more in store for us.

When the nephews found out about Disneyland, it all went down exactly as we had imagined. We watched them take in every moment and tried our very best to stay positive about Georgia.

Julia and I stepped away from the group to talk about the morning and realized that we were in this together. Georgia was both of ours, and so was the pain that came with her disorder. We decided that we'd love on her and have the best possible time we could. We didn't expect much from the day.

Until something completely unexpected happened. It is perhaps one of the most beautiful moments I've had with my daughter since she came into this world.

Julia and her sisters had separated from the group to ride some of the thrilling adult rides mamas don't usually get to enjoy, and I was put on baby duty. To give the kids (and let's be real, the adults) a break, we brought the rest of the group to the Animation Studio in California Adventure. Inside the studio there's a large carpeted room where families can rest their feet from their Disney marathons. The room is lined with gigantic screens. They fill every corner and depict scenes and illustrations from the Disney classics. Every three minutes, the song and movie changes. First you might see Simba and Mufasa stretching across the walls with "I Just Can't Wait to Be King" blaring from the speakers. Next, Peter Pan zooms across the screens while "You Can Fly" plays loudly for the entire room. The room is booming and bright, and all things you'd expect from the happiest place on earth.

We had only strolled in here to take a nap for a beat before heading out to the next big attraction. I was about to close my eyes when I noticed something remarkable.

Georgia lit up.

I was surprised to see my little girl, who often doesn't focus on much, looking all around at the screens. She had a giant smile on her face as the music played. She kicked her legs and made noises! Unless you've spent a good amount of time with our family or with Georgia, you really don't know how much of a miracle this was.

We had gone into that park focusing on Winston's happiness,

assuming there was no way Georgia could experience anything there. But in the end, God had more.

We found something that our daughter actually enjoyed!

What Do *You* Have?

It's easy to resort to frustration or to take things out on others when times get tough. But there is great power in being positive amidst pain. Does this mean shoving things down to a deep, dark place only to have them explode later? No. We should be honest when we hurt, and we should take our issues to God (and others) without fear, as the woman did with Elisha.

False positivity can be even more dangerous than negativity. When Julia and I both pretended nothing bothered us that morning as we fought over every tiny, insignificant thing, we weren't being honest about our circumstances and our pain. However, being honest and being pessimistic are two very different things.

We should express our pain to others and live vulnerably, but we also should be optimistic about the future. It's vital that we expect the *more* that God has for us and look for him in everything.

What I love about the story in 2 Kings, and other stories when Jesus takes something seemingly impossible and blesses it, is God's ability to take something we already have and put his spin on it.

The Gospels tell us of a moment when Jesus was preaching to the multitude. He preached so long that the folks in the crowd got hangry, and the disciples were panicking. If you're unsure of what "hangry" looks like, simply imagine my wife when she needs a Snickers bar ASAP.

When I took my father-in-law out to eat to ask for his daughter's hand in marriage, he only had one word of advice for me. It wasn't "lead her and protect her, you mighty man of God." It wasn't poetic, biblical, or something from an episode of *Parenthood*.

He looked me in the eyes and said, "So, you wanna marry Julia, huh?"

"Yes, sir. Yes, I do," I replied, hanging on his every word, ready for some profound advice.

"Feed her."

Those two words were all he had for me. My father-in-law understood what hangry looked like. You don't want to have to deal with hangry.

Jesus and my father-in-law have this value in common. There Jesus was with a crowd of starving, cranky people, and the disciples told him that they only had five loaves of bread and two fish to feed all five thousand men plus women and children. Any human would look at the scene and panic. But Jesus took what they had, and from that he fed the hungry multitude!

On Disney Day, my handicapped daughter couldn't walk, talk, or ride rides. God took that and still let her experience a bit of Disney magic. Beyond this small moment, God has used Georgia to affect the world. People from all over are constantly praying for, asking about, and learning from our daughter. He took what she is, and with it, he's given our family amazing influence. And he's giving us more and more every day.

What do *you* have?

Chapter Six

WHY NOT US?

BEFORE I MOVED TO THE LAND OF SUNSHINE AND CONCRETE, I spent most of my life in Washington, the land of evergreen trees, constant rain, and, of course, the land of the Seahawks, Mariners, and at one time, the Seattle SuperSonics. To any sports fans, your local teams quickly become part of your identity. This made growing up in Washington hard.

If you grew up in the Evergreen State, you know what this means. Basically, I got used to disappointment. My identity wasn't exactly something to brag about.

In 2008, the Sonics were stolen from us. Before they were stolen from us, they really weren't doing that great. They hadn't won a championship or seen a trophy since 1979.

Yes, we did have the Mariners, but while I lived there, it was sad that a baseball team couldn't win a game to save their lives.

And finally, we had the Seahawks. For most of their existence, the Seahawks were a relatively forgotten team around the country. No one noticed those blue and green uniforms hanging out in the northwestern corner of the country. And since the team began in 1976, they had never experienced a Super Bowl victory.

That was until Super Bowl XVLIII. At the start of their season, the team gathered in their locker room to prepare for the year. This time, things were going to be different. This year, they would make their city and sports-loving citizens proud. They would start things off right. With this force driving them, the team began the season by asking a simple question.

When I heard about this question on ESPN and discovered that it was my team's mantra, it pumped me up for the season too. I found my disappointment in Seattle sports teams fading away, as disappointment was replaced by hope. The question was all about believing in the God-given talent inside of each and every team member. It was the kind of question that has helped many people around the world accomplish something great.

It may have been the most important question of the Seattle football players' careers.

"Why not us?"

"Other teams have won the Super Bowl before us, other teams have tasted victory, so why not us?" the Seahawks asked as they pumped themselves up in the locker room.

If you weren't there, you can't imagine what Sunday, February 2, 2014, felt like. The city was in an uproar, and streets were filled with people. The twelfth man ran rampant amid a green and blue apocalypse. Only, the world wasn't ending. For Seattle, it was just beginning.

Not only did we win the Super Bowl, but also the Broncos barely put points on the board! Peyton Manning, the Hall of Fame quarterback, couldn't touch Russell Wilson. It was hardly even a competition.

Us?

Us?!

All the citizens and loyal fans of Seattle and Washington, accustomed to defeat, couldn't believe their eyes. Then 2015 came, and we watched them make their way to the Super Bowl again. The team who had never played in the big game now found themselves there two years in a row!

We all know the 2015 game didn't go quite as planned, but it's evident the Seahawks' little question had huge results.

AS A MAN THINKETH

You've probably never heard of Puyallup.

It's a little town near Tacoma, Washington, which is a little city outside of Seattle, which is a place you've heard of. It's a suburban sprawl of strip malls and proud home of the Washington State Fair. Most people can't even pronounce its name. Because I know you most definitely do *not* want to be one of those people, here's a helpful tip for remembering:

Step 1: Plug your nose and say, "Pee-ew."
Step 2: Think about your Uncle Al.
Step 3: Point up!

Pew-Al-Up.

As the little boy in *Hook* would say, "You're doing it, Peter!"

In 2004, I moved to this town and took a job as a youth pastor. The first night of our youth ministry, there were fifty teenage faces and hundreds of empty seats staring back at me. Over the course of my time there, we were able to grow the group to one-thousand-plus kids, release five albums, and see countless lives changed. We were blessed every step of the way, and I was stoked about the growth. I also would've been completely happy with things staying exactly as they were. I really had no clue about all the other youth pastors out there with their thousands of kids, Twitter followers, and incredible influence. I wasn't aware of that scene.

I was comfortable staying in my own little world, my small state-fair community—or so I had convinced myself. My bubble was nice and cozy, but I had blinders on. Something was preventing me from seeing how much more God had in store. When you're wearing blinders, you don't see anything other than what you're doing at that current moment. And at that moment, I was a big fish in a small pond. In my church circle and by my church's standards, I was experiencing great success. And that was all I needed.

I was completely unaware of the big movements and powerful stories other pastors around the world were telling. I felt no need to meet these people, befriend them, or learn from them because I didn't understand what they were doing. I would just keep doing my thing in Puyallup. I liked being a big fish. I preached occasionally at camps throughout the year, and I didn't care that they were all part of the same church circle.

Maybe it was a blinder put on by God until the right moment, or my own personal failure to never imagine anything beyond my small community. Either way, it caused me to stay away from the rest of the world. I wasn't really sure what that world had to offer me anyway. I didn't have the desire to join other circles or travel to conferences or meet other youth pastors.

Nah, that's not for me. I'm fine staying where I am.

I don't need this sort of influence. This will never happen for me.

This was my thought until I visited Generation Unleashed. I had managed to venture out of my small bubble to attend a large youth conference in Portland, Oregon. I remember sitting back in my chair with intrigue and excitement. Up until this moment, I had planned to swim in my same church pond. But something was changing inside of me.

I watched thousands of kids sitting in the crowded sanctuary, listening intently to Judah Smith. He was preaching that night at the conference. As I looked on this crowd, vision and excitement stirred up inside of me. I began to see what was possible.

And then I heard God's voice. "To get to where I'm taking you, you need to step out and meet these pastors."

Networking.

It's almost a four-letter word. When I hear it, I imagine that multilevel marketing guy at the party who won't stop trying to convert his close friends to QuickStar. Though the voice of God was not audibly yelling in my ear, I did feel as though he was calling me to do precisely that: to network. He wanted me to talk to pastors whom I felt I was above or thought I didn't need. I felt him nudge me toward stepping out from the back of the building, toward introducing myself.

And step out I did.

We started as acquaintances. After all, we were pastors, so we *did* have a lot in common. Soon I formed friendships with them and found myself enjoying their company, hearing about their churches, their struggles, and their passions. The next thing I knew, I had made some of the closest friends I'd had in a long time. I also found God opening doors and providing opportunities for me to speak, share my story, and learn.

The following year, I preached on the same stage I had seen Judah preach on a year before. I was no longer speaking to the same kids from the same churches I spoke to every year. God was stretching me and opening so many amazing doors.

When I stubbornly saw myself remaining within the same church and the little town whose name no one could pronounce, I was not reaching the people he called me to reach.

There's a short little verse in the Bible that packs quite a punch. It's one of those wise sayings from the book of Proverbs.

"For as [a man] thinks in his heart, so is he" (Prov. 3:7 NKJV).

What if I had thought of myself and my situation differently? What kinds of friendships would I have formed earlier? Who could I have reached and affected sooner?

When we find ourselves thinking small, it's time to shift our perspectives. Instead of convincing ourselves that we'll always be a certain way, it's time to take a cue from the Seattle Seahawks and ask, "Why *not* me? Why can't I accomplish great things too?"

Our Year

Something about being seventeen makes you feel untouchable and unstoppable.

As a high schooler, I had no problem thinking *Why not me?* and acted accordingly. In my mind, I was going to be the guy who made a difference at my school. And so I was. My buddy Andrew and I strolled into that building at the start of a new school year with excitement about what was to come.

My teenage confidence had me believing that anything was possible inside the walls of our school. I wasn't affected by the peer pressure of others or worried that I might get disowned by the "it crowd." I was truly excited to do something meaningful for my high school.

Andrew and I decided to start praying together during the second half of our lunch break. We would scarf down our food then pray to God for our school and our friends. On the first day, it was only the two of us.

"Why not our school, God?" we'd pray.

"You've done such amazing things in other places with other people, so why not us?" we asked, and we believed it. We knew what was possible with God.

A week later, there were three of us sitting at that lunch table.

A month later, there were fifteen to twenty.

By the springtime, a hundred kids in my school cafeteria joined our group halfway through the lunch period. Girls who struggled with anorexia were suddenly eating again, getting healthy, and feeling loved. Guys who were sleeping around, breaking hearts right and left, and feeling broken themselves were experiencing the love and power of Jesus. People's lives were changing in front of our very eyes! The little prayer group that might have been written off as insignificant was having significant results in our school.

I've heard that unbelief says, *Some other time, but not now. Some other place, but not here. Somebody else, but not me,* while faith says, *Anything God did in any other time, he can do now. Anything he did in any other place, he can do here. Anything he did for anybody else, he can do for me.*

That is exactly how our seventeen-year-old selves viewed the world. As a seventeen-year-old man thinks in his heart, so he is.

GIANTS OR HONEY?

There's a story in Numbers 13 about a group of spies sent out by Moses to survey the promised land. As we all know, Moses led the children of Israel out of Egypt and out of slavery. After this, these people wandered in the desert toward the land God had promised them.

God described this land to Moses. He called it "a good and spacious land, a land flowing with milk and honey" (Ex. 3:8). Now back in the day, milk and honey were the sweetest things around. God was telling his people they were in for something pretty great.

Later in the story, however, they arrived at this land, the land of Canaan, and things weren't exactly as they had imagined. They couldn't walk right in, start building houses and roads, and hang a Welcome to the Promised Land sign. The Israelites had dreamed during their desert wandering, and they'd had forty years to do so; but when they arrived, they found people and soldiers living in the land God had promised to them.

Numbers 13:1–2 says that when they got there, "The LORD said to Moses, 'Send some men to explore the land of Canaan, which I am giving to the Israelites. From each ancestral tribe send one of its leaders.'"

So Moses chose his twelve top picks carefully. I like to imagine it like a recess baseball lineup with team captains. They stood there, eagerly hoping to get picked and hear those three precious words.

"I'll take . . . *you.*"

They were the "chosen ones." The few, the proud . . . the *spies*. Their mission: to scope out this supposed promised land and decide if it really was worth all the effort. Moses had given them very specific instructions:

> Go up through the Negev and on into the hill country. See what the land is like and whether the people who live there are strong or weak, few or many. What kind of land do they live in? Is it good or bad? What kind of towns do they live in? Are they unwalled or fortified? How is the soil? Is it fertile or poor? Are there trees in it or not? Do your best to bring back some of the fruit of the land. (Num. 13:17–20)

They had quite a long checklist to accomplish. And off they went with their Milk and Honey–Do List. When they got to the top of the hill, I imagine the land was pretty beautiful. After all, it was created by God for them. Perhaps they pushed past the trees, arriving at the top of the hill, and were greeted by the most beautiful view. Sun setting, bees buzzing, flowers blooming. I mean, if only they had Instagram at that moment: #nature.

The men cut some of the fruit off the branches as Moses had asked. There were grapes, pomegranates, and figs there. The land was obviously rich with resources. It was while taking this precious scenery in, however, that things took a turn for the worse.

"What the . . . ?!" one of them yelled, and the others turned in his direction. Lo and behold, at the bottom of the hill were some of the biggest dudes God had ever created. Gigantic men who would make CrossFit champions look like ballerinas. To make matters worse, these colossal guys were swinging weapons around, just waiting for their next puny victims.

Mo is not going to like this.

When they arrived back at home base, the twelve spies had some negative reports to bring to Moses. Was the land flowing with milk and honey? Yes. But there were also big men, crazy huge men, who seemed to know how to use their weapons.

The majority of the spies only saw an impossible situation. "The people who live there are powerful," one said. "And the cities are fortified and very large" (Num. 13:28). In their minds, it was a lost cause.

But two of the men viewed things differently. Their entire perspective was the polar opposite of the other spies even though they had visited the same place.

"It's flowing with milk and honey! Let's take it!"

It was Caleb, Jephunneh's son. He always had a funny way of looking at things. And I imagine the rest of the group could not believe what they were hearing. Their jaws most likely dropped to the floor.

"Uh, Caleb? Were you on the same trip as we were or . . . ?"

When I think of Caleb, I see him with a big ol' grin on his face, pulling out a piece of fruit from his pocket like a boss. It was probably one of the nice, juicy ones they had collected on the trip. Caleb probably answered, "Of course I was on the same trip! Look at this fruit I found! This place is awesome!"

Caleb was not alone in his excitement. Another one of the spies joined him. His name was Joshua. Joshua would soon become the next leader of the Israelites, helping them to claim their promise. "Caleb's right!" Joshua said. "We got this."

Caleb silenced the people who were shouting in fear to Moses. He looked at Moses and said, "We should go up and take possession of the land, for we can certainly do it" (Num. 13:30).

Two types of people went on that mission and came back with two very different reports. Caleb and Josh saw the honey God had promised them. The rest only saw the giants.

JUST A LITTLE DIFFERENT

It's amazing how two people can view the same situation completely differently. Every spy who was sent out saw an impossible task in front of them, except for Caleb and Joshua. They saw the promised land that God had given them. They saw the ripe fruit and the beautiful scenery, they remembered the promises of God, and they walked up to Moses confidently. They had a "why not us?" attitude.

Let me tell you about a breed of people like Caleb and Josh who are just a little *different*.

Faith people.

Where others see ruins and destruction, faith people see potential. While others might view crack addicts or prostitutes as impossible to help, faith people see what's possible.

Faith people are walking among you, and you may have noticed that they speak a different language. Rather than speak with cynical confidence of impossible circumstances, they speak a language of good report with glaring optimism. They say "giants shmiants" and look for the good that God has in store.

There's a great clump of scriptures in Hebrews 11 that talks about what I like to call the Faith Hall of Fame. "Now faith is confidence in what we hope for and assurance about what we do not see," the chapter begins with a bang (v. 1). Then it goes on to describe the greats.

"By faith Abel brought God a better offering" (v. 4).
"By faith Noah, when warned about things not yet seen, in holy fear built an ark to save his family" (v. 7).
"By faith Abraham, when called to go to a place he would later receive as his inheritance, obeyed and went, even though he did not know where he was going" (v. 8).
"By faith Isaac blessed Jacob and Esau in regard to their future" (v. 20).

"By faith Joseph, when his end was near, spoke about the exodus of the Israelites from Egypt and gave instructions concerning the burial of his bones" (v. 22).

"By faith Moses' parents hid him for three months after he was born, because they saw he was no ordinary child, and they were not afraid of the king's edict" (v. 23).

"By faith the walls of Jericho fell, after the army had marched around them for seven days" (v. 30).

By faith . . .

By faith . . .

By faith . . .

I love the way Hebrews ends this long speech in verse 32. It says, "I do not have time to tell about Gideon, Barak, Samson and Jephthah, about David and Samuel and the prophets." He doesn't even have time to list all the amazing things that have been accomplished by faith!

Are you getting it yet? It's not normal to build an ark when there's no flood. It's not normal to march around a wall and expect something to happen. It's not normal to follow God when you don't quite know where he's taking you. Faith people are *not* normal. But because of their belief in the impossible, God has done amazing things for them throughout history.

So, why not us? This question is important to ask when faced with life's harsh blows.

"She'll never walk. She'll never talk."

When the doctor told us this, we felt a little like the spies scoping out the promised land. I think most couples, when they discover they're pregnant and about to start a family, envision a sort of promised land. They imagine holiday dinners around the table, teaching their kids to ride bikes, and watching their kids graduate college. When Julia and I first found out a baby was on the way, we thought we had an idea of what the promised land of children looked like for our family.

But when we discovered what this land actually looked like, the situation seemed absolutely impossible. We had imagined life going a little differently for us, and the giant of a brain disorder was ruining the life we'd imagined.

It's easy when it comes to mental illness or brain disorders to sit back and say, "Well, that's the way it is. We'll never have a daughter who can do things. Our life won't play out the way we thought it would. We'll just let go of the dreams we had for our family." It's easy to give up when someone's telling us that this ugly thing is always going to be a part of our daughter's personality and identity.

But that would be too normal.

I have learned to get a little weird. I have learned to say "she will" when the doctors say "she won't." God has done it for so many others. He's done it throughout the Bible, as the author of Hebrews proves with the Faith Hall of Fame. He's done it for so many I've personally known, my mom and my dad, my community. God has done it for them, so I believe he can do it for me. Because why not? All the medical answers to this question and all the pessimistic reasons to give up mean nothing when compared to the living God who is more than able and always willing.

I don't know about you, but I'm going to get me some milk and honey.

In Conclusion . . .

Pain may be real, but so is God's ability to pull us out of it. Imagine God to be a bottle of medicine. You read the label to see exactly what it's capable of. On this bottle it reads: "This medicine is always available when you need it. It will never run out. This medicine will not only make you feel better, but also it will leave you with more than you started with. It will leave you with more life, more health, and more vitality. This medicine can be used for any circumstance, ailment, or problem."

This is the type of medicine that everyone would run to the store for. People would stock their shelves with it and turn to it for any and all problems if they knew it existed and worked.

This is how we need to view God. He is the remedy, the answer, the antidote for all we want and need. It's so vital that we understand who God is, because in times of trouble, he's the great provider and comforter and should be the first one we turn to. When everyone is walking out, Jesus is walking in to help us and come through for us. He is a constant source when we need him most.

We see, throughout history and throughout the Bible, God coming through for people again and again. He's the one whom we must look up to, and call out for when we find ourselves in impossible situations.

How do we attain this cure-all bottle? How do we find Jesus, a man who lived more than two thousand years ago? How do we understand the great big God who created the universe?

A remedy means that a solution is possible. It means that you do not have to be stuck in pain and sorrow for the rest of your life. Many of you are probably wondering exactly how to get out of your current situation, or perhaps you're not currently in a situation but want to be prepared when trials come and life takes a turn for the worse.

Action Steps

Here are some steps you can take toward understanding this God, attaining this remedy, and finding a means of freedom from life's pain:

1. Remind yourself that God can be trusted and counted on.

"Trust in the LORD with all your heart and lean not on your own understanding; in all your ways submit to him, and he will make your paths straight" (Prov. 3:5–6).

Start by acknowledging who God is. Revisit stories in the Bible where he frees Daniel from the lion's den or rescues the Israelites out of slavery. Read about Jesus' life and the many times he healed people with seemingly impossible illnesses throughout the Gospels. Also, turn to others to hear their stories. Perhaps you have a testimony of your own that you're forgetting at the moment. Remind yourself that God can be counted on to come through for you in your hour of need.

Then, learn to trust. Trust him to provide for you. Trust him to be on your side every day. Trust him with your most vulnerable moments, with your pain and heartbreak. You'll find him always able to come through for you. There is nothing too big for God.

2. Expect and anticipate good things from God.

God wants to bless your life with good things. Jeremiah 29:11 says, "'For I know the plans I have for you,' declares the LORD, 'plans to prosper you and not to harm you, plans to give you hope and a future.'"

It's time to get optimistic. The pain and trials you might be encountering are not from God. Though he doesn't promise a safe journey, he's not the one inflicting the pain. The enemy is. So what does God have in store for us? According to this verse, some great things. He has a beautiful future laid out, and it involves us prospering and thriving! And the best part? These plans are more than you could ever imagine or hope for.

3. Believe that God is going to more than supersede your need.

A funny thing about God is that he doesn't come in to fix things and then peace out. Yes, he wants to meet our needs. Yes, when we're sick, hungry, or needy, he wants to heal, feed, and provide. But he doesn't stop there. "And God is able to make all grace abound toward you, that you, always having all sufficiency in all things, may have an abundance for every good work" (2 Cor. 9:8 NKJV). His plans for you are plans of abundance.

As I've said, he leaves us with more than we had before. Don't just tweet this thought once and forget about it. It's important to truly believe and have faith that God's not only going to take you out of your dark place; he's going to bless you beyond your wildest dreams!

4. Remember that there's a solution to every problem.

It's easy to think, *There's no way out! There's no hope! How will I ever survive?* when things are really, really bad. But the reality is that for every problem, a solution exists. Sometimes this solution exists in a practical way, such as a counselor or medicine. But often what's needed is something beyond the natural. This is where Jesus steps in. He is the great solution to every problem, no matter how big or small. Time and time again throughout the Gospels, he's healing people with impossible ailments. A man sick for thirty-eight years, a woman bleeding for twelve, these problems seemed unsolvable to the world. But to Jesus, they were solvable. He healed them. He was their solution.

5. Stop complaining about what you don't have. Thank God for what you do have.

Even if your circumstances are dire, I bet you still have something to be thankful for. I could sit and think about all that I don't have and all the things my daughter can't do, but doing so will get me nowhere. The remedy comes when we have an attitude of gratitude. When I thank God for my church, for my family, for my wife, for all the opportunities he's given me, for his provision, for his forgiveness, for his grace, for his unconditional love, for the way he speaks to me and directs my path, I start to realize that this remedy, this God of mine, is already working in my life.

Don't be a whiner and a grumbler, always talking about what you don't have and how awful everything is. No one wants to hang out with that person. Be thankful.

6. Believe that God is alive and real and that he will reward you for seeking him.

What does it look like to seek God? First you must believe that God is alive and real. Then you can practice talking to him, worshiping him, asking him for answers, and spending time with him every day. You can look for him in the Word by reading the Bible and asking him to reveal himself to you. You can also look to him by taking time out to pray.

IN CONCLUSION . . .

Prayer and seeking don't look the same for everyone. You may have your own unique way of doing them. In the same way, listening doesn't always look the same. Some may hear God's voice through pictures. Others may hear a voice in their head or simply have a feeling.

The important thing is not how you seek God but that you do it. This is especially true when you're in need of a remedy or solution. God will reward you and give you everything you need. Matthew 7:7 says, "Ask and it will be given to you; seek and you will find; knock and the door will be opened to you." This scripture reveals that receiving God's help doesn't involve merely sitting back and doing nothing. We must take steps to ask, seek, and knock. We need to do something. He's ready to answer our prayers.

7. Let go and let God.

It's in our nature to want to take control. When a problem arises or a crisis occurs, we want to step into action and control the outcome. But what happens when the outcome is beyond our control? This is certainly how we feel about Georgia's disorder. When there's nothing we can do to affect or control our situation yet we're trying to control it regardless, trouble follows.

We must trust God's hand, direction, and saving power. If we let go of control over our lives and let God take over, we'll find ourselves able to rise out of our circumstances. It's often easier said than done, but we must learn to hand over the reins to the one who has power to affect the outcome.

8. Seek advice.

Similarly to letting go and letting God, we also need to let go and let others help. We're not meant to go it alone, especially in times of trouble. Never be afraid to share with others what you're going through and actively ask for help. Proverbs 15:22 (NKJV) claims that there's wisdom "in the multitude of counselors," meaning the more advice you surround yourself with, the better.

Julia and I have found God most often reveals his remedy to us through people. So many have come around us, praying with us and supporting us during difficult times. Getting advice from close friends and family and looking to your community for help is invaluable.

9. Allow people to love you through it.

Don't stop at advice when it comes to turning to others. Let people love you and be your strength when you need it most. We all need love in our lives. Often people believe that there's no one around to love them, but I've found they are asking the wrong question. They focus on "Am I really being loved?" rather than "Am I really allowing others to love me?"

You need to allow your community and your family to love you when things are bad and when they are good. Don't push people away because you've dreamed up some weird idea in your head about needing to deserve their love. It's so important to let them into your lives when you find yourself in the storm or a rough season.

It's time to replace the weight of your negative circumstances with God's positive reality. He is ready and able to help you when you need him most. I've discussed how he's always available, an ever-present help; I've touched on his ability to leave you with more than you started with; and I've challenged you to realize that he is able. He's done it for others, so why not you?

The truth is, even after discussing all of this, we've barely scratched the surface of the nature of our God. He is a provider, a father, a healer, a friend, a comforter, a helper, and he is so much more. I challenge you to seek out this remedy; look for him in the people of your community; look for him in the Bible, ask, knock, and learn about the only one who can truly turn your situation around.

Part 3

THE REST

It Started with a G

When you're in love with someone, you're consumed. I remember after that first Thanksgiving seven years ago, when I saw Julia dishing up some mashed potatoes across the table, I was instantly obsessed.

I left that day seeing her face in my head, hearing her laughter, and plotting out my next move. There was a surge of excitement and a desire to do anything for her. This is how being in love tends to play out.

But it's not real love. Real love comes after we've just had a yelling match at Disneyland, or after she's hurt me or I've offended her, or while we've both had one hour of sleep and Georgia will not stop crying or throwing up. It comes when, after all of this, I still want to do anything for her and stand with her through it all. True love does not always make sense.

It's hard to expect this kind of true love from multiple people in your life. It's easy to assume that family members and especially your spouse or significant others will stand by your side no matter what. Your best friends may even do the same. However, when you start to think about those friends you see often but only occasionally get deep with, or those friends who live multiple states away and who you may call up once in a blue moon for a chat, it gets a little tricky.

Will they really be there for me? Or even better, *Will they really be there when I don't deserve it? Will they turn up in times of tragedy when I've been a bad friend, or haven't called in a while, or haven't really gone out of my way to mail them a birthday gift or post a photo of them on Facebook?*

Questions like these blur the lines of true love, making it difficult to decide who loves you and who is merely a good friend or acquaintance to have around.

When Julia and I found that we deserved love from our community and friends, they were always there for us. I'm using the word *deserved* very loosely. When you have a sick kid, usually it's those moments of true tragedy and emergency that deserve the attention of loved ones. Not that we're aiming to earn others' love for us by posting photos of Georgia in the hospital or texting our friends for prayer. We've discovered that during the bad times with Georgia our friends and family surround us with support and comfort. And this is amazing. This is, after all, when we really need help carrying the burden.

But what about when things are going relatively well? I'm happy to report that not every day with Georgia for the last three years has involved endless vomit, fifty-plus seizures, and six-hour spells of crying. Have there been days like this? Oh, yeah. But is it every day? Not at all.

Sometimes Georgia finishes her meal, keeps it down, and has zero seizures. Uneventful days don't exactly make for an interesting story packed with juicy conflict. But for some reason, these days can sting a little bit more.

On a good Georgia day, friends and family don't send us messages or run to our aid. And truthfully, we're not asking for this. We understand why they're not there. It's the same reason that I'm not flying around the country to help my friends who don't really seem to need any help at that moment.

But even on her best day, Georgia's brain is still smooth. Even when she's given us a little smile, eaten like a champ, and gotten in some good cuddles, Georgia still can't communicate with us and has an uncertain future. On these days, when there's nothing really to report except for "same-old, same-old," our life feels very much like us and Jesus versus the sickness.

Oddly, it's when things are going well that we tend to feel most alone, as if no one is on our team. We're not upset about it; it's just the truth. This is our weight to bear.

Let me tell you a story about when this all changed.

From the very start, it was evident that our situation was not normal. This was not because our daughter has a rare brain disorder that only occurs 11.7 times per one million births in the United States. The diagnosis alone made her unusual, but it was also clear that there was something about Georgia that people were drawn to. They saw the photos we posted, they read the blog updates about her illness, and they came in droves.

As I've mentioned before, Julia and I were pastors in Puyallup. We had a great community and some really deep friendships. We expected those friends and our families, both very tight-knit, to surround us with support and prayer. What we did not expect was the whole world to take notice and deeply care.

It's easy as a parent to say jokingly that the world revolves around your child, yet I was not prepared for the global impact our child seemed to have. There was really nothing that could have prepared me for the response we got. Yes, at that point in our lives, I had begun speaking at more conferences outside of the Foursquare bubble. Georgia's diagnosis came after I learned to branch out. I already had experienced new, exciting opportunities, and had met more people in the church world. Because of this, I had a good number of people following me on Twitter and other social networks.

Despite all of this, what came after my first tweets to the public when we knew something was wrong was nothing short of miraculous.

The first #prayforgeorgia post came after a service on April 1, 2012. I had told my youth group, United Generation, that we would be going in for testing that week.

So thankful for the prayer tonight at UG, and will definitely be praying for Chad Veach's baby, Georgia. #prayforgeorgia.

The next tweets came a few days later.

Beautiful baby girl is going to become an even more beautiful woman of God. Doctor's faith will be stirred today. #prayforgeorgia.

And they continued, with more "believing for full healing" and "God IS able" encouragements. Before we even walked into the doctor's office for the diagnosis, we had a swarm of support on Instagram. But for the most part it stayed pretty local. Until April 10. On that day, though we faced the most difficult news, we were also floored by how many people seemed to genuinely care about our situation.

People from all over the world deployed the hashtag #prayforgeorgia. Social media celebs and people I'd never met told our family that they were praying and believing for a healing miracle. I remember even Joel Houston, who at the time was starting Hillsong New York with my friend Carl Lentz, wrote, "This is a fight I'm up for." We could feel the love.

A couple of weeks after the diagnosis, I was invited to speak in Australia. It was my first big trip since the situation went down, and I remember how hard it was to leave.

I had debated even going, because I had this new heightened sensitivity about our situation. *While I'm away will something worse happen? Will she have her first seizure? Will she make it to see tomorrow?*

It was the first true glimpse of my new reality. I had this desire to adjust my whole life because of Georgia, but this made little sense. Besides a lack of development, Georgia had none of the other symptoms yet. Julia and I decided early on not to let this illness control us, and to still live life to its fullest.

I kissed my wife and daughter good-bye and said one more prayer. On the plane, I got choked up thinking about what I would say from the platform about what we were going through. *Will I even be able to get through this?* I wondered. *Should I ignore it and speak about something else?* But how could I ignore it? My world had been flipped upside down.

Upon arrival at the church, again I was astounded by how many people knew about Georgia and were already praying with our family.

"We're believing with you for a miracle," they said.

Here I was, halfway around the world, meeting people who had Georgia on their minds, who were praying and believing that her life would get better.

Georgia was no ordinary baby. People were endeared and moved by her, seemingly drawn to our struggle. Strangers wanted to tell her story. Perhaps she symbolizes faith, hope, and love to people. As I've said, Georgia's life continues to reveal the nature of God to me. It has taught me about believing despite the circumstances, about trusting and changing my perspective. It was also teaching something similar to those around the world. We were all learning from Georgia.

This initial reaction—others helping to carry our burdens—floored us, and we truly felt it and were grateful.

It felt like a loud choir, singing and booming in our ears, "You can do this!" But that choir didn't sing every day. And in the months and years following, on days that were average or even good, the silence seemed deafening. Because we had so much to compare it to, we felt alone in a large stadium. We tried not to think this way, but we sometimes felt as though our cheerleaders had abandoned us. We were the ones responsible for praying for Georgia. If we didn't pray every day, we couldn't guarantee that anyone else would.

But these stadium seats didn't stay empty.

On a trip out to New York to speak at Hillsong, I got a glimpse of a different type of support and love. On a previous trip a few months before, I had met Joe Termini. The first thing you need to know about Joe Termini is that he's an Italian New Yorker with a big personality.

The first weekend we met it was instantly a party. He knew all the best spots in the city—the newest, hottest restaurants—the people we had to meet, and the places we had to go. He was our own personal New York tour guide. We hit it off and stayed in touch after that weekend.

Our friendship was still relatively new when I found myself back in New York months later to speak at the church. So I was shocked when, after a service when we were hanging out together, he looked at me and said, "We're gonna go out. We're gonna get marked together."

There we were sitting in a restaurant in Brooklyn. It was late. I had just finished preaching the entire day at multiple services, and my new friend was looking at me, sincerely, New York Italian passion raging in his eyes.

That Sunday I had told countless stories about Georgia from the pulpit as I often do. I had talked about Diagnosis Day and Seizure Summer, about God's grace to us, and about how we believed in a future for our daughter.

Our story was a platform to communicate who God had been for Julia and me during this season. I had opened up about my ups and downs, using it as a vehicle to reach people and relate with them. I had laid it all out there, and as always, I wasn't exactly sure what the response would be.

Are people tired of hearing this? That sort of thought flashed through my brain, but I usually tossed it aside.

Will people come up afterward and ask me a million questions? This often happened after I talked about Georgia publicly.

"So, what is lissencephaly? What are the treatments? Is there any hope at all for a cure? Have you given any thought to having an in-home nurse?" At churches, people often swarmed me with questions like these. I answered the best I could, even though I'd rather not go into the details of the strange disorder or get someone else's nonmedical medical advice.

But the response following this service was different.

My friend Joe ran up to me as I stood talking to people near the stage. Mirroring what Joel Houston had said many months before, he told me, "Hey, I want you to know that we're in this fight together." A statement like that felt good to hear. It seemed as though he really cared.

"Thanks," I replied, thinking that his supportive words would fade away or make me feel good just for a moment, like a tweet or a text message does. I didn't think it would be something that would stick with Julia and me through the bad *and* the good days. At that moment, I still believed it was Julia, me, and Jesus versus a brain disorder. I felt that though people cared and prayed for us, they really couldn't fight this fight with us. It was our war. Though I would never admit it at the time, looking back, I realize I had convinced myself that we were alone and that only a family member could show us real love.

But Joe Termini would not take "thanks" for an answer. He

wasn't looking to get his sound bite in and run. There was a plan brewing in his eyes, something more than a supportive comment. And I'm not going to lie: I was scared.

What exactly does this crazy New Yorker have in store for me? Are we going to take a trip of some sort? Is he going to go beat up a doctor for me and try to change Georgia's diagnosis or something? I wondered what exactly this crazy Italian had planned.

"Let's meet up. Tomorrow morning. I know a great place we can get pancakes. See you at nine," he said matter-of-factly.

Pancakes seemed harmless enough, so I agreed.

The next day he took me to Five Leaves, opened in Heath Ledger's memory, and we crushed a stack of pancakes. Then he drove me somewhere unexpected.

We parked and walked over to a tattoo parlor. I had never gotten a tattoo before. I always liked the way they looked, but I never really had an itch for one. Tattoo parlors weren't exactly part of my day-to-day lifestyle.

"We're getting a *G*," Joe said, as we stood outside the door. "For Georgia." He looked at me with that same sincerity. This was him proving what he'd said the night before. This was him saying, "We're in this fight together."

Joe had never gotten a tattoo either, but he had designed some Gs for us to get during our visit to the tattoo parlor. They were both simple, but each was different.

"Okay," I said to Joe. This would be my first tattoo, one celebrating my daughter. It made perfect sense. I was excited to celebrate her life with this act of love. But I still couldn't understand why Joe would want to get one too. I couldn't wrap my head around why this friend, one I'd only known for a little less than a year, wanted to get a tattoo with me.

We walked in and got marked with my girl's initial.

As I sat in the tattoo shop, I became overwhelmed with

emotion—which, obviously, I didn't let out. (I mean, I was getting a *tattoo*.) But inside I was overcome with a sense of Joe's love for me.

At times Georgia's problems can seem so impossible, so never ending, and here was a friend showing me in a profoundly permanent way that he was fighting right by my side. I don't know if I had experienced loyalty quite like that before.

My relationship with Joe drastically changed that day. He will now always have a symbol on his arm that represents my daughter, my struggle, and his faith that God has a greater plan for us.

The next time I saw Joe in New York, something felt different. Unlike other relationships, I didn't feel as if I had to question where I stood with him. There was no "Are we cool?" or "We still friends?" Rather, I felt overwhelming security and confidence in our friendship.

Because he was marked.

Julia and I never could have imagined or believed what happened next. I don't think Joe could have either. Somehow that single letter and the tattoos that Joe and I got together sparked a movement of support for Georgia and our family around the country.

I remember golfing one afternoon and getting a group text from three close friends. These three had been close to us for years. They were among the first posting #prayforgeorgia and surrounding our family with support. They had journeyed through life with Julia and me. They had been there since the beginning.

"You're not going to believe this!" I yelled on the course as I excitedly shoved my phone in my friend's face. In the text was a picture of three wrists with the letter *G* on them. Our friends Roman, Erika, and Karen had gone out and shown us their love and support. They got marked for us too.

Within weeks we saw Instagram photos, received texts and phone calls, all about people getting the G-tat. People all over were permanently marking themselves to show their love for our daughter.

The G-tat officially began to spread.

Soon we found that celebrities and athletes were being moved by Georgia's story and getting the G-tat too. The support was overwhelming. Football players tagged the letter *G* and dedicated their seasons to Georgia. There was one player at the University of Houston who's a good friend of ours, and in his season as a starting quarterback, he began every game by putting the *G* for Georgia on his cleats.

There was another football player for the University of Washington whom I'd been meeting with for a few months. When you're first getting to know someone and trying your best to be a mentor, it can be hard to know where you stand with them. *Am I getting anywhere? Does he understand that I love and am here for him?* These are the questions I often ask myself. I really loved this kid, but I wasn't quite sure where our friendship was until one day when I got a text from him. He had gone out and gotten the G-tat too. No more questions necessary.

Another time while in Sydney at a conference, I spent a week hanging out with one of my favorite players in the NBA. As I've stated before, I'm a bit of an NBA fanboy and basketball fanatic, so I was pretty stoked to spend time with him. I found that not only was he amazing at basketball, but also he was a great guy. We had an awesome week together, but I was not expecting what happened next. He had heard all about Georgia, and we had discussed her a bit during my time with him. But I was shocked when I learned that after we parted ways and he headed back to LA, the first thing he did when he landed was go out and get a G-tat.

There were no words. It seemed clearer and clearer to Julia and me that there was something about Georgia. It was something that had nothing to do with us.

One weekend Julia and I flew down to Palm Springs with Georgia and spent time with a close friend from LA and his girlfriend, who happened to be starring in a popular TV show at the time. We ended up hitting it off with this actress, and all of us had a great weekend. Usually when you hang out with new friends, you don't really expect them to be "kid people," especially if they don't have kids. But this girl wanted to spend the entire trip chilling with Georgia. She seemed to fall in love with her and bond with her. To our surprise, when she got back to LA, she went out and got a G-tat too. One of our closest friends went with her and they actually got the tat together!

The movement grew, and the platform got bigger.

Strangers came up to me when I was traveling. I remember one trip when I was at a mall and a group of ten to twelve sorority girls from Tennessee ran up to me.

"Oh my gosh!" they said. "We follow you. We love Georgia! We're all gonna go out and get the *G* together." I had never even met these people, yet they were going to get a tattoo for my daughter! It was all very surreal.

Today, more than fifty people have a tattoo with my daughter's initial, and the number is still growing. Just a few months ago, my brother and sister-in-law went out and each got one. The support is overwhelming, to say the least. It appears that Georgia is contagious. People love her and continue to express that they love her and are standing with us, believing for a miracle.

Suddenly, our stadium is full. Because a tattoo is permanent, it means there are tons of people telling us they are in it with us through the good and the bad. On days when Georgia can't keep a meal down even with the feeding tube, these people have a *G* marked on their bodies. They still believe that God has a bigger plan. On days when Georgia is doing well—when she smiles, makes fun sounds, or enjoys a trip to Disneyland—they have the

G marked on their bodies. They're still saying, "Hey, we know it could be even better. This fight is not over. We're with you no matter what."

The G-tat has become such a beautiful symbol of real love to our family. It expresses a support like none we could have ever imagined. When the images of Gs marked on wrists and arms were sent to us again and again, I suddenly remembered the prayers I had prayed over Georgia in the womb. "God, let her have a global grace." The world felt the effect of Georgia, and Julia and I had to stand back and receive this crazy outpouring of love.

We had not done anything to deserve this permanent sign of loyalty. It's not as though we were striving to make a social media campaign. We weren't enlisting a marketing team, sitting around a boardroom table, and asking, "How can we make this thing spread? How can we make Georgia the face of lissencephaly? Oh, I know! We'll start a tattoo. Yep, a tattoo. That will do the trick, and everyone will get them. It will be *huge*."

We weren't trying to work our relationships, rubbing elbows with other pastors at parties, passing out images of Georgia, and asking them to spread the word.

There was nothing we had asked people for; we were simply receiving and resting in their amazing love and support.

They were loving us.

We were doing nothing.

Period.

Chapter Seven

THE LANGUAGE OF LOVE

Have you ever been in love?

If your answer is no, then you're a liar. I've heard that the average person falls in love six times in their lifetime. Six times! That is a *lot* of falling in love. What is to blame for this embarrassing statistic? I believe it must be a combination of bad parenting and listening to too much Mariah Carey or Boyz II Men as children.

If you've experienced this Boyz II Men kind of love, then you know it's awesome. You also may know a little something about the special languages that come with romance. No, I'm not referring to nicknames like "babe" and "hun." I'm referring to . . .

The Five Love Languages.[1]

That's right. If you weren't aware, someone sat down and decided that all of us as humans have five ways to communicate love. And, actually, out of these five, each individual typically has two primary ways that they either give love or receive love. Here's a breakdown of the five:

Number One: Quality Time (also known as Julia Veach's gold-star favorite)

This love language happens to be more like a *foreign* language to me. Apparently it refers to time when you and another individual just get together and . . . spend time together.

That's it.

That's the entire activity.

You just *be* together.

"I don't feel like we spend enough time together," my wife always says as we're sitting *right next to each other*.

I respond with, "Babe, we sleep in the same bed. We work at the same place. What do you mean you need more time? I don't know if I have more time!"

NUMBER TWO: WORDS OF AFFIRMATION

This one I can get on board with. Basically, it's when someone tells you . . .

"You are wonderful."

"You are awesome."

"You are attractive."

"You is kind. You is smart. You is important."

Compliments are still in style, people.

To find someone illiterate in this language, look no further than Backhanded Compliment Guy. Backhanded Compliment Guy is not winning, and when Words of Affirmation is among your top two love languages, Backhanded Compliment Guy is your worst nightmare.

One night after a church service, I actually ran into this guy.

"Oh, my gosh!" he said to me. "You preach *way* better now."

To which I so wanted to respond . . .

"Shut up! You listen better now. How 'bout that, huh?"

But instead, I smiled politely with my teeth clenched.

And now, we come to my other personal favorite love language . . .

Number Three: Physical Touch

This one is pretty self-explanatory, so I don't need to spell it all out for you. Basically, if you want to love me, just touch me and tell me how great I am. This is my love language.

Number Four: Gift Giving

The Gift Givers are people who freak out at Christmastime and feel no guilt when they break the bank to buy the perfect gift.

You know the ones.

They knew the family Secret Santa name drawing had a twenty-dollar maximum, but they bought everyone iPads anyway. If your family has a token Oprah who likes to reenact the Favorite Things episode every December 25, then you understand this language.

"You get an iPad mini, and you get an iPad mini. EVERYBODY GETS AN IPAD MINI!"

Alas, we arrive at the final love language. This language is spoken by the individuals who tend to cry if someone thinks to do the dishes or clean the toilet without being asked. They are incredibly touched whenever someone offers a helping hand and cleans up around the house or does yard work. It's a language spoken by moms around the world.

Number Five: Acts of Service

Forget presents, hugs, time spent sitting around a room just being together, or nice frilly words: people expect you to be there to help them move into their new house and would love if you offered to pick them up from the airport.

I don't know about you, but I think there's a missing love language. There can't only be five, right? Another language exists out there. Julia and I experienced it first with Joe Termini. We've all seen it, and it looks something like this:

The words "I love Mom" cascading down a forearm.

Something in Hebrew etched along the center of a lower back.

A flock of birds on an ankle, a shoulder blade, a wrist. (Really, you could put a flock of birds anywhere, and people would still find a way to make it meaningful.)

Half of a tribal symbol stretching across a chest with the other half on that person's best friend's chest.

Anchors. Roses. Chinese characters. Sleeves and sleeves and more sleeves!

Ladies and gentlemen, I give you Love Language Six: Tattoos.

Tattoos have become a sign of loyalty, love, and endearment in our culture. Getting inked can often communicate to loved ones that "we're in this together" or "we're family." It can also communicate that not everyone thinks things through before they do them. I mean, we've all seen some terrible tattoos out there.

I'm on a personal mission to find the worst tattoo in the world. One day I was in the lobby of a hotel, and a huge NFL-lineman-looking guy was standing in the line next to me. Marked down the side of his massive arm was none other than . . . a Wi-Fi symbol. I thought to myself, *There's a candidate.* Was he trying to say, "I love the Internet"? Or was he saying that he's really connected to the world around him? The world may never know.

When on vacation with my dad and brother in Palm Springs, we were all chilling in a hot tub. Another guy who was staying at the hotel was sitting with us. We spent twenty minutes together, swapping stories. He was a nice guy and seemed pretty normal, until . . .

He rose out of the hot tub to reveal a giant tattoo on the middle of his back.

"What was this tattoo depicting?" you ask.

Well, a clown, of course, with balloons floating up across his back and flying into his shoulder blade.

Candidate.

The worst of the worst tattoos aside, I think we can all agree that a tattoo is pretty serious.

You may be surprised to discover that this sixth love language is not a revolutionary new idea. I actually believe that God originated it. That's right, Hipster Bearded Man, you did not invent the tattoo or like it before anyone else. God actually went out and got ink first.

Isaiah 49:16 wonderfully communicates God's thoughts toward his people. It says, "I have engraved you on the palms of my hands." And that was written in 740 BC, so . . . it's kind of like the first tattoo ever.

I had read this verse many times before, and though it did often fill me with warm Christian fuzzies (oh, God loves me, yay!), I didn't quite grasp what an extreme act of love this was until I had my own encounter with tattoos. Because of the G-tat and Joe and many others' acts of love, tattoos—something I had never really wanted or thought too much about—became a very important part of my life and the Georgia journey.

It was a new kind of love and commitment, and I have been completely overwhelmed by the outpouring of this sixth love language.

THE REST

Some time after the G-tat experience with Joe, I read Isaiah 49:16 again. It is such an amazing message from God to his people. God is speaking not only about engraving his people on the palms of his hands, but also on the hands of his Son. This verse comes from a portion of the Bible that foretells Jesus Christ's life, death, and resurrection. God would soon give his only Son and, on the cross, put permanent scars on his hands.

A tattoo of us.

"I have engraved you on the palms of my hands."

As I read this verse again, I feel the same overwhelming emotion I had at the tattoo parlor with Joe. It's funny how God continually uses my daughter and the reaction of my community to reveal something about his character to me. He went out and got marked for me. Not only that, but he marked his Son for me.

I mean, he's like *obsessed* with me.

He's so obsessed that he put me on his hands.

When you're the creator of all things, your hands are pretty important. They represent power and compassion. They're what you build things with, create things with, reach out and hold things with.

"Father, into your hands I commit my spirit." These were Jesus' words in Luke 23:46 as he breathed his last breath on the cross.

Hands are a trusted, sacred place, and right smack-dab in the middle of God's are what else but my initials!

And not only did God get marked for us, but he also marks us and writes on us to reveal that we are part of his family. In Jeremiah 31:33, God says, "I will put my law in their minds and write it on their hearts."

I like to imagine God as a frat boy who's super pumped about his new tattoo. "Look, I got one! It's you!" I imagine him saying that and then following with, "Hey, let's mark you too!" In his excitement, he gives everybody tats to show that we're all in this together.

"I will be their God," the verse continues, "and they will be my people."

God knew us and had us written on him before we were even born. Then he went so far as to send his Son to die for our sins, and he marked his Son for us. Finally, to show us that we are his people, he marked us and wrote his promises, his hope, and his love on our hearts.

It's hard to wrap my mind around how people I'd just met or strangers who only knew me through social media were getting tattooed in solidarity with me and my family; but even harder to understand is how a great, awesome God who's perfect in every way went out and ruined his perfect hands with my initials. All I've ever done is wrong him, yet he put me in the palm of his hands. Let me invite you into my internal dialogue with God.

Uh, God, why? What's wrong with you? Why would you do this? When did you do this?

Was this when I signed up for that conference?

Was it after I Instagrammed my daily devos?

Was it when I first stepped into a church building?

Was it when I tithed regularly?

You probably regret this decision, don't you? I mean, a tat, that's like . . . permanent stuff.

I grew up in a subculture of churches in the '90s that I tend to blame for internal conversations like these. You may have experienced the same or simply watched something similar from the outskirts. It was a culture that often shouted the phrases, "You gotta chase after God!" or "You need to get ahold of him!"

So try to "get ahold" of him I did. I read my Bible. I prayed with my eyes shut extremely tight. I didn't do drugs. I didn't sleep around.

"Am I ahold of him yet?" I'd ask.

It was all about striving. *What can I do to reach God so that he loves me? What do I need to give to God to earn his favor?*

It was all lies.

Paul put it this way: "While we were still sinners, Christ died for us" (Rom. 5:8). The answer to my questions regarding when God drove out to the tattoo parlor for me is right there. He did it while I was screwing up, before I ever knew him. Basically, all of my devo-Instagramming means nothing because he already loves me and has loved me since the beginning.

I know that it's hard to fathom, but we don't take the first step. He does. It took me a while to finally learn that Christianity is not about doing stuff; it's about receiving God's great love.

Just as when I'm around that crazy New Yorker whose audacious love removed all questions about our friendship, there's no need to be insecure around God. We can be confident that he's in this for the long haul. As 1 John 4:18 says, "There is no fear in love. But perfect love drives out fear."

We can be 100 percent confident and secure in Christ Jesus' perfect love language. Forget words of affirmation and physical touch; we're talking about the language of a God who sacrificed everything for us while we were still ugly, broken, dirty, and bad people.

Because of this, we don't have to be afraid. Can all the Christians who have been killing themselves by spending 80 percent of their time apologizing to God, living in shame, and feeling rotten breathe a sigh of relief now?

And in . . .

And out.

That's better.

To those who are highly task-oriented, you may be having a small panic attack now, thinking, *What's my job, then? What am I supposed to do?!*

It's simple. Just rest.

We never have to guess. We never have to question. He loves us. He's together with us on this.

When it comes to my little one's life and the stormy seasons, it's easy to feel as if toil would get me out of my circumstance. *Maybe if I just prayed one more prayer while she was in Julia's womb she would've come out healthy and happy. Maybe if I fast more God will heal her. Maybe if I spend half of each day on my knees he'll come through for my family. Maybe if I hadn't made so many mistakes, this never would've happened.*

But God didn't give me a sick daughter because I lost his favor in some way, and working around the clock to earn his favor will not get her out of this situation. I have to learn to rest and trust that God not only has me written on his palms, but he also went out and got his own G-tat.

I have a friend who plays for the Seattle Seahawks. In the spring of 2013, he came to me before the season started and told me about a team scrimmage he could invite friends to. He gave my family passes to watch this scrimmage, and my wife and I, being pretty huge fans, were stoked.

Seattle gets about three days of sunshine a year. The day of the scrimmage happened to be one of those days. All signs were pointing toward an amazing time watching a pro team play in the sunshine. Everything was perfect. So I grabbed my family, and we headed out to the practice facility.

Three plays in, I watched my friend score a glorious touchdown. In that moment I lost my mind. I was completely freaking out, talking about people's mamas, throwing up gang signs, and doing church chants. I really didn't know how to behave in this setting. It was my first scrimmage, after all.

You see, it wasn't just that my friend had scored a touchdown. It was *how* he had scored that touchdown. Our quarterback, Russell Wilson, got behind center. "Hut, hut, hike!" he yelled as he hiked the ball. And there went my buddy, racing straight at the defender. He took one jab step to the left, got his defender to bite, then went right. He separated and caught the pass, then ran straight down the field. It was amazing. One move like that and he shook off the defender, completely losing him!

I bet some people today think the same thing can happen with God. They believe that one little move can separate them from him.

Some assume that one moment of weakness, one moment of sin, or one mistake can shake God loose. But that is not true. Nothing you can do can put you out of God's grace, blessing, and unconditional love. That's why they call it unconditional. Even when you are faithless, Christ is faithful.

I am convinced of this love God has for me. Paul wrote, "For I am convinced that neither death nor life, neither angels nor demons, neither the present nor the future, nor any powers, neither height nor depth, nor anything else in all creation, will be able to separate us from the love of God that is in Christ Jesus our Lord" (Rom. 8:38–39). Nothing I can do or have done will separate me from the love of my father. It's time for you to be convinced of this love too.

Chapter Eight

WHERE DO I GO?

THE THING ABOUT PROBLEMS IS WE ALL HAVE THEM. EVERY now and then, life throws us a little "situation." You've experienced them. "Situations" are moments that seem so colossal our brains shut down, and we don't know where to turn.

We've all experienced the total terror that comes when we find ourselves in a city we're not familiar with, walking around with an iPhone trying to find our destination. That moment when you have the address all ready to go, you have no idea where you are, and your battery life is at 3 percent—now that's a situation.

Where do you go? What do you do? Just curling up in a ball and crying somewhere sounds like the best plan, but you have to explore other options.

When Google is the answer for *everything*, and Google won't load in the time it takes your battery to run down, where else can you turn? (Not that I completely understand this sentiment. I'm not exactly the best Googler. What takes me thirty minutes to track down, my wife could find in thirty seconds. But I do recognize it plays a pretty vital role in the rest of the world. Moving on . . .)

Looking back on all my "situations," both good and bad, one particular predicament comes to mind that not even Julia's best Google skills could've helped.

While on a trip in Houston, Texas, with my buddies, we decided to play golf. "Let's make this a competition," my buddy said. "Whoever wins, wins a hat."

I looked around, scanned my competitors, liked my odds, and said, "In."

I'm proud to say on that day that I was the Tiger Woods of Friendly Hat Golf Tournaments. While reveling in my victory, my buddy drove us over to a hat store. I had a plane to catch, so I had to make my selection fast. Straight from the store, I'd be heading to South Beach, Miami, to speak at my good friend Rich Wilkerson Jr.'s youth conference. It was going to be a great time at a conference where two thousand young people gathered to worship. I mean, Rich's youth ministry was hot stuff, and I'm thinking, *I better look goooood when I show up.*

As I walked into the store, I saw it.

The perfect hat.

It just screamed South Beach.

I saw it and visualized myself wearing it while taking a selfie with LeBron James. It had palm trees on it, was a perfect fit, and— the best part—it was free and basically screamed "winning."

I got the hat. I got on a plane. I flew down to Miami. Unfortunately, I was running a little bit late to the conference. But no big thing, because . . . I had my new hat on. It would all be okay.

I remember strutting into the building that night like a boss. I walked down the congregation aisles, saying hi to all my pastor friends.

"What up?! How you been?"

Then I arrived at my chair that read "Reserved for Chad Veach." All in all, I was feeling pretty important.

The soulful pipes of Israel Houghton were leading the group in worship that night. I love me some Houghton and some worship, so in my South Beach hat swag, I started singing along.

"Holy, holy, ha! Get it."

The music was on, and I was into it, closing my eyes, raising my hands. Until . . .

"Excuse me, Pastor Chad?"

Someone from behind tapped me on the shoulder.

"Pastor Chad, do you realize what your hat promotes?"

I was confused and a little bit bothered by the interruption. I gave him a quick nod and said, "Yep. Go, South Beach!" And then went back to worshiping.

"Holy, holy, ha! Get it."

"Excuse me, Pastor Chad?"

It was him again. I turned around.

"What?!"

"Pastor Chad, do you realize that your hat promotes marijuana?"

What? No. Who? How did you?

I took my hat off, looked down at it, and saw . . .

Marijuana.

Hello, predicament.

What I had thought were friendly Miami palm trees were . . . not. Marijuana leaves were all over my newly won hat. Suddenly I had flashbacks of the friends I had waved at as I strutted into the church building only moments earlier. I looked around the room and wondered . . .

How many of these two thousand young people now think that I'm all about the grass?!

Where do I go?

I'll tell you where I went—straight to the bathroom. I threw the hat in the trash, wetted down my hair, and tried to stroll back into the church as if nothing had happened.

Maybe nobody noticed.

On the way back I saw another good friend, Pastor Chris Durso, standing near the entrance of the church. "Chris, you're never going to believe what I did," I said.

He looked me straight in the eye and said, "I know, man. I saw you walking in with a big grin on your face and thought, 'What an idiot.'"

We all have problems. Some of them come in the form of weed-covered hats, while some of them are more massive. They may come in the form of a sick family member. You may have received a phone call that your mom or dad, aunt or uncle, or niece or nephew doesn't have much time left. You may be coping with a tragic reality.

You may have never experienced death or sickness but instead faced problems in your relationships. Maybe a friend betrayed you or someone you thought you were going to marry and spend the rest of your life with suddenly changed his mind and walked out on you.

Perhaps you've experienced losing a job that you needed. You might find yourself not knowing where your rent money will come from or how you'll put food on your table.

Where do we go when problems like these hit?

WHO TOUCHED ME?

There's a story that I love in the book of Mark that tells us where two different people with two very huge problems went when things seemed impossible.

One of these individuals was Jairus, a desperate father with a very sick daughter (sound familiar?).

The other was the Woman with the Issue of Blood. I know, it's a terrible name. Somehow this woman is part of one of the most epic teaching moments of Jesus' life, yet she still goes down in history as "the Woman with the Issue of Blood." Very catchy, King James. Rolls right off the tongue!

For the sake of brevity, we'll call her WWTIOB.

Before we get into WWTIOB, let's talk about Jairus. Jairus was *somebody*. He had clout, a nice home, people who worked for him, an Escalade, tons of followers. He knew and experienced what it was to have a good life. Typically, for a man like this, solving problems is a piece of cake. And for Jairus it often was.

Until one day he found himself in a situation that his status couldn't get him out of. His daughter, at the age of twelve, was on her deathbed. He had imagined so much for her life, and now he found himself preparing to say good-bye.

He had heard rumors of Jesus, the reports on Facebook and Twitter. You know, the general hubbub of Galilee circa 1 BC. This guy seemed to be healing cancer, the sick, the lame all over the place. People were talking about his power, so Jairus knew what he had to do.

The only way my daughter can be healed is through Jesus, he finally resolved. But Jesus typically walked among large crowds, and Jairus had no way of carrying his dying daughter all the way to him. He had to figure out a way to get Jesus to come to his house.

He grabbed his Moleskine and began to write:

How to convince Jesus to come heal my daughter.
By Jairus

Option 1: Offer him money.
Option 2: Offer him a job.
Option 3: Play the desperate dad card.

Jairus stared over this list. Option 3 was really the only option. From what he had heard, Jesus wasn't into the money thing and he had a full-time gig as a carpenter.

Option 3 it was. Jairus gathered himself, kissed his daughter good-bye, and made his way to Jesus. It was his only hope.

When Jairus finally found the crowds, he pushed his way toward

Jesus. Upon reaching him Jairus fell to his knees and begged Jesus to heal his twelve-year-old. The response he got as he wept into the dirt was not at all what he had anticipated. Calmly and collectedly, as if he knew this would be happening all along, Jesus answered, "Yeah, sure."

Jairus looked up through his tears. *Wait, what?*

"Sounds good, 100 percent. Let's go get your daughter."

Well, that was easy.

Jairus wiped his tears, stood up from the ground, and dusted himself off. "You serious?" He had to double check.

"Absolutely," Jesus answered. "Which way are we walking?"

Jairus freaked out. He started texting his wife. "Babe . . . *hand clapping emoji* *cry smile emoji* *cat head emoji just for fun* . . . You're not going to believe it. Our daughter is gonna go to high school. She's gonna graduate! She's gonna get married . . . well, we'll see about that one. But it worked, babe! We're coming home now!"

It was as they walked to Jairus's house that the WWTIOB entered the picture. She was sitting on the side of the crowd, waiting for something, anything, to rescue her from her awful situation. I should probably tell you how WWTIOB got her name. This woman had been bleeding for twelve years.

Can we all agree that twelve years is a long time? To understand how long it is, I want you to think about what you were doing twelve years ago. Think about your clothes and the music you were listening to.

WWTIOB had been bleeding for twelve years with no solutions. She had spent all her money on doctors and naturopaths, and she was only getting worse.

I've found that typically when this story is told by rock star preachers around the world, this is the moment when the preacher says, "You know what, guys? It's just like us! We try everything else but God. Jesus was her last resort!"

But this was WWTIOB's first encounter with God. We can't say it was her fault she hadn't been healed because she didn't know of anywhere else to turn until that day. And in her first encounter with God, she provides a perfect example of how we should respond in life's trials.

She was sitting there in her hopeless, desperate situation, and for some reason, Jesus caught her eye. For some reason, she instantly knew. *This is the answer to my problem. This guy I've heard about. He's the only one who can help me.*

So she threw her hoodie over her head, then made her way through the crowd in stealth mode to grab his garment. The Bible says she came up behind him in the crowd and touched his cloak. What a ridiculous, simple act. I mean, just touching him? That would never work.

But just like that . . . she was healed. She was free. It was all too good to be true!

Jesus froze in his footsteps and started yelling like a crazy man. "Who touched me?! Someone touched me! Who was it?"

It may have been the most socially awkward situation ever. But I guess when you're God and you created the universe, there's nothing you can't handle—not even social awkwardness.

"Who touched me?" he yelled again.

At this point, the disciples were a bit concerned. They whispered to the crowd as they gently tried to push Jesus on his way. "Sorry, guys. Jesus has been preaching *a lot* this week, and walking on water and stuff, and there was that legion ordeal . . . he really needs a nap and a cup of coffee. So we're just gonna go now . . ."

"Who touched me?!" Jesus continued.

"It's fine, Jesus. You're gonna be okay. Calm down, and let's go to Jairus's house."

"Nope, not moving. Somebody touched me. Who touched me?"

One of the disciples chimed in, "Hmmm. Jesus, can you phrase that a little differently? Maybe you could shout something else next time? People are starting to stare, and well . . ."

"Who touched me?!"

Suddenly, the woman fell down on her hands and knees before Jesus. She was completely vulnerable, waiting to be reprimanded for touching such a powerful person.

"It was me."

Jesus didn't respond with a yell. He didn't berate her or lash out at her for inconveniencing him. He looked her right in the eye. It was a beautiful moment—the kind that requires a background keyboard player and some strategic lighting and wind.

He looked at her and gently said, "Daughter, do you realize it's your faith that made you well today? It's that you trusted in me and believed in me. Go and live in peace."

In the midst of this beautiful, keyboard-playing moment, as doves seemed to fly through the air and perfect Jesus looked deeply into the woman's eyes . . . a group of #haters came charging through the crowd.

It was time for Jesus to meet the worst friends in the world—Jairus's friends.

"Jairus, your daughter's dead, man."

That was their opener to Jairus, whose heart sank.

"Let's leave this guy alone. Come back home. She's dead. Yep, dead, dead, dead. Can't get much deader."

Jesus, in the midst of his touching moment with WWTIOB, whipped his head around to face Jairus. "Don't believe them. Don't fear, okay? Only believe."

Jairus didn't know what to do. *Could he really bring her back to life? I mean, I did just see him heal this woman. But raise someone from the dead? Is that even possible?*

Jesus started to walk, and Jairus, along with his terrible friends, followed. They arrived at Jairus's house and were greeted by a *situation*. We're talking an all-out scene. Women were weeping and wailing. Everyone was dressed in black. Jerry Springer was there.

Geraldo was there. Everyone was already talking about Jairus's daughter in the past tense.

"Oh, she was so sweet."

"Oh, she always had the nicest smile."

Jesus had to silence the noise, the quitters, the naysayers, so he could hear the voice of God. There was no way he could perform a miracle with the criticism and negativity that was in Jairus's house.

"Everybody out!" he yelled.

Once everyone cleared out, Jesus looked to Jairus. "Where's her room?"

Jairus pointed him in the right direction. As he followed Jesus to his daughter's room, he suddenly found his faith growing stronger and stronger. *I think he can and he will do this!*

Jesus entered the room where the twelve-year-old girl was sleeping. And he woke her up. She was healed.

Two people.

Two massive problems.

Two equal conclusions: Jesus is the answer.

POSSIBLE WITH GOD

When life throws the giant sick-kid, endless-illness kind of problems at you, what are you supposed to do? In the age where everything is an Internet search away and it seems so easy to find answers, dealing with the impossible can get downright frustrating.

We make lists; we sit and crunch numbers. I know that my wife and I have done this.

Well, if I save money on coffee each month, we'll be able to afford better treatment.

If we get Georgia into physical therapy, then maybe her brain will start developing. Maybe we'll get some results?

We reach for solutions like these, and when they fail, we have a whole new set of problems. *Physical therapy doesn't work, God! That new treatment failed us just like the last! What next?! Where else is there to turn?*

Most of my life I felt as though solutions were pretty easy to come by. Like Jairus, I had it pretty good. Amazing parents, amazing siblings. Money was never too tight at our house. There were no major deaths around us. We went to church. We had faith in God. I could often solve things by talking a problem out with my mom or dad.

But a solvable problem is different from an unsolvable problem. When Julia and I heard "She'll probably die at the age of ten" and "She won't develop past three months," where were we supposed to go from there? According to the doctor, it sounded as though giving up and riding out this disorder was our only option.

An easy place to turn at this time is toward faith. But it would be of no use if I simply turned to my faith for solutions. Thinking things such as, *Because I've always believed in Jesus, I deserve to see a miracle for my daughter* would get me nowhere.

No, that would be turning to myself, my actions, or a sense of what I deserve in my time of need. I want to be a believer who builds my faith on Jesus alone, not my own works. I desperately need to fall on my knees in front of him because he's my only hope. Where else can we go for answers?

It's simple. It's Jesus.

Ephesians 2:8–9 says, "For it is by grace you have been saved, through faith—and this is not from yourselves, it is the gift of God—not by works, so that no one can boast."

WWTIOB couldn't walk around town saying, "Look what I did! I was sooooo good at being a Jesus lover that I got healed! Look at me! I'm awesome!" She couldn't do that because she didn't *do* anything. She simply received Jesus' healing.

When life deals you problems, you have to go, run, and fall at the feet of Jesus. Let him be a part of the reality of what you're going through. He's not afraid to hear about your issues.

It's often easy when we sit with our problems all alone, rehearsing them in our heads, to think somehow we're too weird for Jesus to handle. *No, he wouldn't want to help with my issues. He'd rather heal someone of cancer or solve world hunger or something.* This thought pattern can reinforce the belief that you're the only person who struggles with a particular issue because you don't share it with anyone, especially not Jesus.

But it's during these moments when we're feeling all alone in our trials that we need Jesus the most. We're missing all that he has for us.

In my situation I've definitely had those same isolating feelings—that my issue is too unsolvable, even for God.

It's easy to feel weird when I'm out in public with my daughter. I'll be standing in line at Starbucks, and the sweet lady behind me will look at G lying in her stroller and say, "Oh, how cute! How old is she?"

"Three," I'll answer. This lady will try to play off her startled reaction with a worried smile. My daughter is now at the age where she's obviously too big for a stroller. People can no longer assume that she's only a baby. The disorder is starting to show, and in public it can often be isolating.

This is the real stuff, the stuff that can make you feel very alone if you go to no one for help. That's why I choose to go to Jesus. I've learned that there's nothing too weird or impossible for him. He's *literally* seen it all.

Because my faith is in Jesus, because I turn to him and lay this situation at his feet, I believe he is going to heal my daughter.

The beautiful thing is that he's not going to heal her because I can quote scripture like nobody's business or I put money in an envelope every Sunday. Isn't that reassuring? I can simply rest. God's going to heal my daughter because he is a good God, and because he is *for* me.

He's for you too—for all of us. That's why we can't let our circumstances determine how much we believe this fact.

Jesus put it this way: "What is impossible with man is possible with God" (Luke 18:27).

Where are you going to go with your weird, impossible, twelve-year-long, never-ending, seemingly hopeless situation?

I know where I'm going.

In Conclusion . . .

Turn to Jesus, the one who has engraved you on the palms of his hands, the one who loves you no matter what, and rest in his love. In times of trouble, he is the one who can be trusted to help. But how exactly do you do this?

"Turn to Jesus" is a phrase repeated in churches right now. "It's all about Jesus." "All you have to do is turn your eyes upon Jesus, and he will take care of the rest." "Just point people to Jesus, and he will help them." These statements are beautiful and true, but what exactly do they mean? Jesus lived more than two thousand years ago, he died on a cross, and I, along with other Christians, believe that he rose again and is still living today in each and every one of us who believes in him. This means we can communicate with him and experience him even today.

We understand this Jesus through reading about him in the Bible and the Gospels, which give an account of his life and the words he said. We can also experience him through the Holy Spirit, whom he sent as a helper to us. Turning to Jesus can mean physically opening this Bible and reading his truths, or it can mean praying and calling out to Jesus to talk or ask for help. If you ask him, you will be able to experience a relationship with him, one in which you can hear his voice, experience his power, and see his miracles in your life.

If turning to him involves actions of seeking him, talking to him, and reading about him, then why call the entire encounter "resting" in his love? Don't these actions inherently involve "doing" something?

The reason resting is such an important concept for the modern Christian to grasp is because though there are some actions we can do to spend more time with God, none of these involve earning God's love. We cannot earn God's love because he already gives it to us freely. He doesn't love us more if we talk to him more, read our Bible more, or post Instagrams of our devotions more. We were already engraved on his hands before we did anything, and he continues to love us no matter what. However, we can miss out on this love, we can completely ignore the point, if we don't turn to him and receive it. That's where the doing comes in. Rest in his love. Receive it. Run to him like the woman with the issue of blood. Run to him, and he will help you.

Action Steps

Here are some important truths to remember and actions you can take as you practice resting in God's love during difficult times:

1. God loved you long before you loved him.

You did not initiate the relationship. You may have turned to him or asked him to be your Lord and Savior, but it was not you who made it happen. God created you, and he sent his Son to die for you before you ever did a single thing. Rest in the fact that he is the initiator and that he chose you before you did anything.

There's no regret when it comes to God. He doesn't regret sacrificing his Son for you. I don't know about you, but sometimes as a human who deals mainly with other humans and their flaws, this is a difficult concept to grasp. But when you do grasp it, you'll discover how beautiful God's sacrifice is.

2. Be convinced of God's love and grace even when you don't feel "it."

Sometimes as Christians we wait for that experience, that vibe, that sense that God is with us and loving us. This does happen. You may be in a church service or praying in your car and suddenly feel "it." You become so overwhelmed with the reality of God's love and grace. In this moment, you may find yourself crying or overcome with emotion.

But feelings come and feelings go. Don't let feelings dictate what you know about God. Don't let the emotions of one day change how you understand God the next day. God will never change despite how you may feel. He loves you, and he has grace for whatever you are going through and whatever you've done.

3. Don't turn to quick fixes that simply fill a void. Turn to Jesus who heals our hearts.

This can be difficult to put into action, especially because we all get so used to our bad habits. Rather than talk things out with someone who's hurt us or ask Jesus for wisdom, we watch a game or put on a TV show to drown out the problem and try to ignore it.

Or maybe instead of turning to some distraction like social media or sports, we want the easiest solution possible. We look for the quickest way out of our problem. Jesus wants to heal our broken hearts, he wants to physically heal our bodies, and he wants to pull us out of the mire. How do we know this? Just take a look at his life and the years he spent healing those he encountered. He's able, and he's willing to help. But don't immediately turn to other fixes. Let him be the first one you call.

Because he is all-knowing, he already knows your situation

and is dying for you to turn to him. He loves to help you through whatever impossible mess you've found yourself in. Know that you can turn to him for any and every issue. Pray, ask for help, have faith that he will do it, and you'll see amazing miracles take place.

4. Think about the good things God has done for you and recall all of his blessings.

The past has the ability to give us faith for the future. In the midst of your storm or your trouble, if you can pause and remember all that God has rescued you from, you'll find yourself more confident that things will turn out for the best. If you can remember previous trials you've experienced and the way God intervened and rescued, you'll have more faith to face your current situation.

Not only has he helped you time and time again, God has also blessed you. Think about your life, the people who are in it, the family you have, the work you do, the provision you have, the shelter you have, the country you live in. Think about these things, and view them differently. They're not only part of your life; they are blessings from God. This will give you faith for tomorrow.

5. You don't have to earn God's love because you already have it.

I've already touched on this, but I'll say it again. Reading your Bible more, praying more, going to church so many times, dropping so many dollars into the tithe bucket—these steps don't earn God's love.

Though it's great to do all of these things, they are not what get you the love of God. God already loves you. Before you were ever born, he loved you, and he loves you today.

Some face trials and think that they're being punished by God in some way. This prevents them from turning to him and receiving love when they need it most. This is a lie from the enemy!

Don't push away from God's love at the time when you most need to draw closer to it.

6. Confess God's love and peace over your situation.

There's great power in physically speaking words about God's love and peace when you're going through something. If you believe that he can help and that he is able to calm the storm, you can speak it.

But don't just confess good things to him alone. Tell them to others. Tell your friends, your community, your coworkers, your church, and your followers what you believe about what the Bible says. Practice saying things out loud. It might seem awkward at first, but with time, you'll get better and better. You know that God loves you. Now, it's time to tell the world about it!

7. You're at your best when you're at rest.

When we're frustrated because something is not happening by our own strength, we tend to take it out on others or ourselves. If we're trying really hard on our own and it's not working out, we can snap at our family or beat ourselves up about it. This happens when we're viewing God's love as something that must be earned. If we feel as though we have to strive to earn this love every day, we'll only get mad at ourselves when we continue to fall short.

But if we rest, sitting back and thanking God for this unconditional love, we'll find ourselves filled with more peace and happiness. The more I learn to rest in God's love, the more I find that I'm at my best. It affects my whole life—my work, and the way I interact with others and my family. Don't settle for frustration, anxiety, and worry. Rest in God's grace and love.

Christianity is not about doing and striving to attain something. It's about receiving. Just as Julia and I didn't do anything to deserve or attain the support and love for Georgia from our community or those around the globe, we don't have to strive to attain love and support from God.

In the previous sections, we established who God is and what he can do for us when we find ourselves in the middle of stormy seasons. But what do we do next? How do we respond to this ever-present remedy? Do we push to gain God's favor, hoping that he will pull us out of our circumstances?

No, we simply receive his love. His overwhelming, unconditional love is better than anything we could ever dream up. It fills us with peace, it rescues us even from the darkest of places, and the best part is that it's freely offered. We can attain it without a price.

Don't push, strive, and torture yourself, constantly focusing on your failures and missing the love God has for you. Rest and see what happens.

Part 4

THE BETTER

"Let Me Tell You a Story . . ."

What exactly gives me hope for the future? What about my circumstances makes me say, "There is hope for Georgia"?

As I sat down to write a book about stormy seasons, the low and tragic blows of life, I wanted so badly to find the answer to this question. I was hoping to give you a happy-twist ending. I so desired to tell you a story about Georgia's miraculous healing that occurred while writing out the chapters of this book. I wanted the reader to read this and say, "Wow, God healed Chad's daughter!" or "God's giving him signs and improvements every day showing that Georgia will indeed be healed! God can do the same for me!"

And hopefully, by the time you read this, this will be the case. Georgia will be healed, and our family will have a miraculous testimony. But for the moment, I must put my current situation down into words.

To answer this question about what exactly gives me hope, I tried to compose a list of material. Where can I milk the miraculous out of this story of mine? This question drove me to write the following:

1. Georgia smiled at me yesterday.
2. Georgia went an entire day without having a seizure.

3. I put my finger up to her hand, and she squeezed it for a moment longer than normal!

4. When I talked to her, she made eye contact with me for a few minutes.

5. We took a picture of Georgia today, where she looked like a beautiful toddler and not like a "special" kid.

This was about as far as I got. I sat, staring with frustration at my list. *There has to be a number 6, right? Come on, Chad! Think!* The list seemed a little pitiful, and the whole exercise completely pointless.

This is where I get really honest with you, reader. I stared at my list, wondering, *Do I even have a story here? Will this inspire people to turn toward God in their hour of need? Should I even tell this story when I'm still waiting for the miracle that comes at the end, that big finale?*

I suppose the average church lady could look at this list and spot some miracles and victories. "Oh, the Lord does work in mysterious ways. New mercies every day!" she might say, trying to make me feel better while waving her hand in the air toward heaven. But it's more likely that the average person would look at my list and get downright depressed.

"*These* are your miracles? Really? You're going to have to try harder than that, Chad," he or she might be tempted to say.

And it's the truth. In my vulnerability and honesty as a pastor who travels the world proclaiming God's goodness from the pulpit, when I look at this list and at my daughter, there is really nothing about my circumstance alone that gives me any hope. Hope certainly doesn't come from Georgia making cooing sounds or holding my finger, because although she's doing those things, at three years of age she's still unable to talk to me or walk. Hope doesn't come from the doctors' reports and recommendations.

They never offer us a way to get out of this—only ways to cope, to ease the seizures, to calm the aspiration, and to extend Georgia's life and survival a few more years.

And I know this is true for many people's trials. For many, like me, there doesn't appear to be a light at the end of the tunnel. When you look at your situation, whether it be illness, divorce, or death, it's hard to see a reason to hope.

So why believe? Why have hope? Why write a book to tell the story of my struggle?

Aside from the outpouring of support from social media and the many people running out to get the G-tat for Georgia, something else made our circumstance unusual.

When the diagnosis first occurred, I put my faith cap on. I continued to speak to my youth group and, as I mentioned, even went on international trips. I had to proclaim that God was going to heal my daughter. Being a Bible-believing person, I knew that Jesus was capable of doing exactly that.

I also knew our community would believe it too. I knew from the moment that we sent out the tweet and told our friends and family about Georgia's diagnosis that they would pray for a miracle and say, "We're praying with you!" or "God is able!"

This would have been normal.

But I found that people surprised me. As with the G-tat, I was floored by the confidence with which people were approaching me and talking about Georgia.

I would find myself at a conference or church, and people would come up to me and say, "God told me your daughter is going to be healed."

One time a woman came up to me with a serious expression on her face. She was not messing around when she looked at me and said, "I had a dream last night, and in it Georgia was completely healed. She was walking and talking!"

This is *not* normal.

I'm sure those of you in the church world have experienced the occasional person coming up to you and saying something like this over your life. My favorite overuse of the phrase "God told me" in the church world comes when a desperate young man or woman approaches someone of the opposite sex and says, "God told me that we're supposed to get married."

If you've found yourself in church as much as I have, you know that people like to abuse those three words.

"God told me you're a terrible pastor."

"God told me you're supposed to be my personal mentor and meet with me seven mornings a week."

"God told me to stop eating yogurt."

If you aren't a churchgoer, I'm sure this sounds even more nutso crazy.

It would have been easy for me to cast this woman's words aside or write them off as crazy Christianese. But the number of times people came up to me and told me confidently that my daughter would be healed made the idea hard to shake. Even people I respected and believed to not be psychotic were saying similar things to me.

"God will . . ."

"He told me . . ."

"I had a dream . . ."

"I had a vision . . ."

"When I was praying, he showed me . . ."

". . . that Georgia will be healed."

One time would be easy to ignore.

Three times, even, would be easy to forget.

Fifty to one hundred times, though? Something was up. It seemed God was trying to tell me something.

One instance stands out to me more than others when

thinking about these declarations over my daughter. A pastor approached me after a speaking engagement and told me a story. To understand the impact of this story, you first need to understand the type of healing stories people typically hear.

I'm sure you've heard some before even if you've never stepped foot in a church building. You've probably seen someone leap out of a wheelchair in a YouTube video or heard someone give a testimony of being healed from cancer during a service. In your own church, you might have heard people tell you that they no longer need to wear glasses because God healed their vision. Or even when you study the Bible, you read about Jesus healing the lame, the lepers, the diseased, and people who had been sick for many years.

According to doctors, lissencephaly technically is not a sickness; it's a disorder. A doctor wouldn't say that my daughter is sick, but rather that she was born this way, that this is who she is and was meant to be. It's easy to hear things like this and assume that this will always be the way things are. God doesn't come in and transform someone's brain, making that person a completely normal, functioning human. Or does he?

Though I had faith for Georgia's healing, this perspective of who she was meant to be and the disorder-versus-illness thing was hard to shake off. But then I heard the story from a pastor and it suddenly shifted my thinking. It was about a little girl. She and Georgia had a similar diagnosis. The little girl had not developed properly and couldn't walk or talk.

At three years of age, she was healed! I was hanging on every word as I heard how she began to walk and talk despite her condition. It was a miracle!

"Excuse me?" I wanted to respond. I was full of shock. Up to that point, I had never heard of a miracle happening in a situation like ours. The pastor said that he believed this would happen for us, that we, too, would receive a miracle. He told me that he believed Georgia would one day walk and talk.

It could happen, because it had happened.

This story filled me with a new kind of hope. I was inspired to continue praying for my little girl and to ask others to pray. Not that I didn't believe God was able before I'd heard this amazing story. I truly believed Ephesians 3:20, that God was capable of doing "immeasurably more than all we ask or imagine." But this particular story gave me more hope that things could change.

And I rode the wave of this hope during the course of the next year. This story, the image of a girl running and talking to her parents at three years of age, carried me. I often visualized Georgia's third birthday. I imagined us gathering around her, singing "Happy Birthday," and watching as she suddenly lifted her head and looked around. I imagined her running into my arms and Julia and me grabbing her and crying.

And then her third birthday came. Julia and I were tempted to let the day pass by without saying anything. For us, birthdays often sting more than other days. When Georgia turned one year old, we barely wanted to celebrate it. Not because we don't love our girl or because we don't want to celebrate her life. Birthdays have always been difficult because they're reminders of another year passing by with no development.

Her first birthday was definitely the roughest. Our house was packed with friends and family, we had Georgia all dolled up, we sang to her, we gave her the cake, and we proceeded as though everything was normal. But everyone at the party knew it was not normal. It was the giant elephant in the room. Georgia wasn't going to be grabbing her cake and shoving it into her mouth. She had no clue what we were celebrating or that we were celebrating at all.

We tried to let the second birthday slide by unnoticed, but our family threw us a little get-together. It was quiet, nothing too big to draw attention to another year.

But the third birthday was rougher. Probably because of the miracle story. I knew deep down that God works differently in each person's situation, but I still wanted to have faith. I still believed that if he could do it for another family, he could do it for us. I still woke up with a small glimmer of hope. *Maybe this could be the day. Could our stories end up being even more similar?*

I woke up and said a prayer to God. I asked again, probably for the thousandth time, "God, heal my daughter."

But on her third birthday, nothing happened. Georgia did not walk or talk or run into Julia's and my arms. It was just another day.

When people read stories like mine, they're probably wondering, "Chad, exactly where does your hope come from?" Because the truth is, even though her third birthday was heartbreaking, even though the miracle still hasn't come, I still have hope. The miracle story contributed to it, as did others I've heard since Diagnosis Day.

Let me tell you another.

I have a close friend in New York City named Chris. Chris has two beautiful kids, and one night he called me up in a panic. His son had gotten sick out of nowhere. All of a sudden, the sickness had turned deadly and dangerous for their boy. With worry and trepidation, he and his wife rushed their boy to the hospital.

When they arrived, things didn't look good. Their son's blood count was dropping at a rapid rate. One word describes the scenario for my friend: *frightening.*

I could hear the fear in his voice when he called. "Chad, I don't know what to do. They're not sure if he's going to make it. What do I do?" His voice was shaky and at times even hard to hear. He was not hiding that he felt completely helpless.

Like the Georgia situation, he had his entire church praying for his son at that moment. People from his congregation were sending him texts, saying, "He will be healed!" They were all asking God for help and belief.

But the doctors didn't think there was much hope for their son. The reports were grim, but they were going to try a few different procedures before giving up.

When this all went down, I was in LA with a good pastor friend of mine. To understand this story, you need to know that this friend is a bit of a character. He has a big, booming voice, an infectious smile, and you never quite know what he's going to say next. I adore this man because, simply put, he cracks me up.

Aside from being hilarious, he's also one of those faith people. Remember them? They're just a little different, because they believe in the impossible. They don't panic when times get rough but instead say, "Yep, God will do it," with complete confidence.

So when my friend called me out of desperation and I was standing right next to a faith person, naturally I was anxious to hand over the phone.

I turned to him before passing the phone and said, "Look, I know you don't know my friend in New York, but I believe you have a gift of faith. Would you mind if I passed this phone over to you? Would you mind praying for my friend's son who is in the hospital, who doctors are saying has no chance?"

The man agreed, so I put the phone on speaker and held it between the two of us. "Chris," I said, "I know you don't know this person, but I've asked him to pray for your son. Is that okay?"

"Oh, absolutely," Chris said. At this point, it was clear that Chris was ready to try anything. He was desperate for a miracle.

My friend in LA leaned in to talk. I closed my eyes tight, ready to focus intently on his prayer and agree with a few "amens." But a prayer did not come out.

"Hey, Chris! Let me tell you a story."

My eyes popped open in confusion. *What?* I thought. *It's not story time. I didn't ask you to tell a story. I asked you to pray.*

He continued, "It's about someone I know in El Paso, Texas. He's also a pastor."

I'm sure my friend was a little thrown off at this moment, and if he wasn't, then I certainly was. He was in a hospital room, most likely having to talk to nurse after nurse. He didn't exactly have time to hear stories from a man he'd never met before about a man he'd never met before. But my friend in LA continued to talk, in spite of my facial expression.

"This man also had a son in the hospital," he continued. "His situation sounds like yours. The man had his entire church fasting and praying for his son. They weren't eating, instead spending their days asking God to heal the boy. The doctors told this man that his son would not make it. They said he would need to go through tons of procedures and, even after going through those, he would most likely not survive. But people still prayed. The very next morning after his discussions with the doctors, when things seemed absolutely hopeless, his son was suddenly healed."

Once he finished his story, he finally started his prayer. But there was something different about this prayer. It wasn't a simple "By your stripes we are healed, Lord" or "We ask for a miracle."

He spoke into the phone with authority. "God, I pray that what happened in El Paso, Texas, would happen in New York. I pray that just as that boy was healed despite what the doctors said, so would Chris's son be healed."

He finished his prayer, and I turned off the speaker on my phone.

"Chris?" I said. But no one replied on the other line. I panicked that he hadn't been listening to that entire prayer. That would have been awkward.

"Chris?" I said again. And then I heard weeping.

"Thank you for having him pray for me," he finally said. I tried to give my friend some more encouragement before hanging up. The strong sense of empathy that had formed because of my journey was rising up in me again. I wished I could have done something, anything to protect Chris and his family at that moment.

Then I looked over at my friend, the man of faith, and asked him, "Why did you tell him a story before you prayed?" It seemed so unusual to tell a story instead of jumping right into a prayer. I was curious why he took this approach.

What he said would probably sound like gibberish to most. It certainly did to me. He said, "I told him a story because *the presence of God abides on the ark of the testimony.*"

"Come again? Pastor, I have no idea what you just said," I replied bluntly.

He said it again, only slower. "Chad, the presence of God abides on the ark of the testimony." My face was obviously blank, so he expanded on his point. "When you tell a story of what God has done and accomplished, his presence comes and the impossible is possible."

The next morning, I received a phone call from Chris. Again, he was weeping, but this time it was for a different reason. He was taking his son home from the hospital. The doctors couldn't explain it, but his boy was healed and healthy.

It was a miracle.

And my pastor friend had countless stories like this. He had traveled around the country preaching and praying over people for healing. He always told a story before he prayed, and many times he saw people miraculously healed of their sicknesses.

His words inspired me. Julia and I had been praying for Georgia almost every single day of her life. Up to that point, we hadn't let a day go by without asking God to begin developing her brain. We had a lot of faith, but did we have hope?

The spark of hope the miracle story had ignited in me was fanned by Chris's situation and my friend's call to remember the stories and to tell them before we pray. Though we've seen dark days and experienced a good share of low moments, I believe that God can do this and that he is able.

When I look at my list of hopeful moments with Georgia, yes, it tends to look a little bit depressing. But when I add to that list all the other reasons to hope, I see that Georgia getting better is possible.

1. Georgia smiled at me yesterday.
2. Georgia went an entire day without having a seizure.
3. I put my finger up to her hand, and she squeezed it for a moment longer than normal!
4. When I talked with her, she made eye contact with me for a few minutes.
5. We took a picture of Georgia today, where she looked like a beautiful toddler and not like a "special" kid.
6. A little girl began to walk and talk at the age of three, even when doctors said it was impossible.
7. God healed the son of the man in El Paso, Texas, after his church fasted and prayed.
8. God healed my friend Chris's son when things looked bleak.
9. Jesus healed the woman with the issue of blood (Luke 8).
10. Jesus healed a man who had been sick for thirty-eight years (John 5).

And the list goes on. The truth is that there's not enough space in my journal or memory on my iPad to jot down how many stories there are proclaiming that God is able. And these stories, for me, are reasons enough to hope.

Julia and I are banking on the fact that God is the same yesterday, today, and forever. When we hear stories about God miraculously developing little girls' brains or bringing little boys home healthy after a life-and-death illness, "yesterday" doesn't seem too far away. It doesn't seem like a distant Bible story unreachable for modern-day people. Yesterday, God healed Chris's son. Yesterday, God healed a little three-year-old girl. Today, he is still able.

If we put our hope in stories like these, we know that there's something a whole lot better than throw-up laundry, avoided birthday parties, and endless seizures waiting for us. We're ready for that better.

Chapter Nine

WHO MOVED MY HOPE?

We're always waiting—waiting for Nike to release the latest and greatest Air Jordans, waiting for likes and comments on our most recent posts, waiting for the latest iPhone model.

Even as we walk out of the store, proudly holding our iPhone 17 plus (or whatever model we're on now), we're eagerly waiting for the next iPhone release. It doesn't even matter that whatever we purchased last week is already obsolete. We can't wait for that new phone! Will it be black or gold? Will it be bigger or smaller than the last one? Will it be round, square, or rectangular? Gah, we can't wait!

There's something powerful about knowing something better is around the corner waiting for you. That next job promotion! That exciting new opportunity! That girl you met last week ("Could she be the one, Lord?"). That new baby you Instagrammed!

These are the *good* things that keep us up at night. I don't know about you, but I'm happy that it's not always "How do I pay the bills?" or "How will we ever get out of this financial mess?" or "When will this sickness go away?" or "How do I get along with my crazy family?" that keep us from sleeping in the wee hours.

Sometimes we lie awake actually dreaming about what's coming next.

Anticipation is a beautiful thing.

"It's a boy!"

I remember hearing these words from the ultrasound technician and being filled with excitement. A boy! I immediately imagined one-on-one basketball games in the driveway and watching football games together on Sundays. Yes, these words were amazing.

But they could not compare to the words that came next. Julia and I had asked our doctor to run a few more tests on baby number two, so we could learn more about him. You probably could only truly understand how amazing these next four words were if you've experienced parenting a sick child. The doctor looked at us with a smile and said . . .

"Your baby is healthy."

When we found out Winston was going to be a strong, healthy little boy, Julia and I were overwhelmed with anticipation. Those nine months were perhaps the most exciting months our family had ever experienced.

"We're going to have a kid who's healthy! He's going to run! He's going to make eye contact! He's going to laugh at our jokes. Well, he'd better laugh at our jokes! He's going to graduate high school! He's going to get married! He's going to live life to its fullest!"

I remember sitting up at night, thinking about it with such happy expectation. What would he be like? I would get to watch my son grow. I would get to be his friend, his father.

After the devastation we had experienced during the course of the last couple of years, the nine months of waiting for our healthy boy were sweet to the soul. While coping with our daughter's diagnosis and condition, we had experienced so much pain and even a little bit of shame.

Though deep down I think we knew it wasn't right to do so, Julia and I would still often wonder, "Did we do something wrong?" or "Could we have prevented this?"

We even went through genetic testing to see if it was our fault our daughter was the way she was. I remember Julia reading Internet article after Internet article to see what she might've done during pregnancy to hinder Georgia's development. Did she not take enough prenatal vitamins? Did she not get enough sleep? We were walking through life, carrying the weight of something that wasn't our fault.

But the anticipation of a healthy, smiling, growing Winston began to lift that weight. We felt our souls healing and our home becoming filled with more and more joy each day over the course of those nine months. The best part was that when Winston finally arrived, the anticipation didn't go away.

First we discovered what he looked like: dark hair, round face, and just about perfect in every way. I mean, you thought *your* kid was cute! Next we anticipated his first steps. Today we're waiting for him to say more words and form sentences. Soon I'll get to carry on a conversation with my son!

When it comes to Winston, we're always waiting for the next amazing thing, because we know that his milestones can and will happen.

WHAT IS HOPE?

I have a friend named Michael who, when he was in high school, went on a mission trip with his dad to Africa. While there, something tragic happened. He contracted a terrible disease that affected his kidneys. Since high school, he has been in and out of the hospital, been on dialysis, and has even been pronounced dead a few times. All in all, it's been a terrible battle.

One day when I was in his neck of the woods, Michael and I got a cup of coffee together, and he told me something he felt God was speaking to him: "You have so much faith in who I am and what I can do, but you have no hope for your situation."

He proceeded to tell me how God was dealing with his hope. He told me that he believes anyone who has faith should also have hope, but that many people are missing this key life ingredient.

But what is hope? Why is it a key to our lives? Why do so many of us forget about it?

I remember Michael describing to me how hope is excitement for the future. He described it as a substance that we need today in order to make it into tomorrow. Almost like food, sleep, and water, it carries us through the day. It's the Winston-anticipating, standing-in-line-for-twelve-hours-for-the-next-iPhone feeling—a belief that something even better is waiting for us.

The dictionary definition of *hope* is "a feeling that something good will happen or come true." The word *will* is key to the definition. When you have hope, you don't think *maybe* something good will happen or *wish* that something good will happen. You have a feeling that there really is something better in store for you.

I love the way G. K. Chesterton, a Christian apologist and author, put it. In his book *Heretics*, he said:

> Hope is the power of being cheerful in circumstances which we know to be desperate. It is true that there is a state of hope which belongs to bright prospects and the morning; but that is not the virtue of hope. The virtue of hope exists only in earthquake and eclipse. . . . For practical purposes it is at the hopeless moment that we require the hopeful man, and the virtue either does not exist at all, or begins to exist at that moment. Exactly at the instant when hope ceases to be reasonable it begins to be useful.[1]

It is during our most troublesome moments, when the sky seems to be falling around us, that we need to cling to hope the most. When it doesn't make sense, we must look "cheerfully" at the future.

As I sat at the coffee shop with my friend Michael, he continued to explain that he was learning how often he found himself having only faith—a belief that God was a great God who sent his Son Jesus and who forgave our sins—but not hope. "Now don't get me wrong;

faith is a great thing to have," he said. "But what about hope? I've been trying more and more to be a man of faith *and* hope."

I walked away from that coffee time feeling extremely challenged. Here I was, a pastor and a father with a very sick daughter. I had been traveling around the world proclaiming who I believed God was and proclaiming these truths over my daughter. "He did it for Abraham, Isaac, and Jacob. He can do it for me!" I'd shout these truths from the pulpit with passion.

And I believed it! Faith has never been a huge struggle for me. I truly believe that God is willing and able to help.

But where was my hope? Did someone move it? I swear it was around here somewhere.

As I drove away, I began to ask God, "Do I have hope? Do I have expectation and anticipation that something better is coming for my daughter? Am I certain that things will work out in the end?"

In a letter to the church at Corinth in Greece, Paul wrote these words: "These three remain: faith, hope and love" (1 Cor. 13:13). Since the beginning of Christianity, faith has been a key concept. After all, you have to *believe* to be a Christian. Love is also central. "For God so *loved* the world." "Love is patient, love is kind . . ." Paul ends 1 Corinthians 13:13 by writing, "The greatest of these is love."

Yes, not every church everywhere does a perfect (or even good) job of communicating these important truths, but for the most part, faith and love have seriously shone in the spotlight of church history.

Hope, on the other hand, has been the redheaded stepchild. Somehow along the way it has been lost in the mix.

THE AUDACITY OF IT ALL!

In 2008, when Obama was running against McCain, I remember standing in the aisle of a bookstore when a book caught my eye. I saw

Obama's smiling face on the cover. The title instantly grabbed my attention: *The Audacity of Hope*.

Audacity.

It's almost an edgy word. It means daring, bold, risky, rude, presumptuous, having nerve, and gall! If you're audacious, then you're living life on the edge and unafraid of the consequences.

Obama was almost trying to answer the public's questions, such as, "How dare you hope for good things in America?" or "How dare you have hope for your race or for minorities to have a voice in politics?" Simply by using the word *audacity*, Obama was making a very interesting comment about hope.

Hope goes against the public opinion. It can even go against common sense at times. It assumes risk, and in a cynical, negative world, it's not always the popular choice. Perhaps that's why we champion love and faith while hope slips through the cracks.

One story in the Bible stands out when I think about the audacity of the belief that something good is coming up no matter what the circumstances.

Let me tell you about Audacious Abraham.

When it comes to edgy, this one-hundred-year-old knew where it's at. Yeah, that's right. Abraham was one hundred years old when God fulfilled his hope. That, my friends, is *old*. And his wife, Sarah, was a whopping ninety! We're talking *Jeopardy*-watching, in-bed-by-7:30 p.m., purple-haired *old*.

But it was during these golden years, when most people give up and wait for death, that God decided to give Abraham something. Many years before this, God had told Abraham time and time again that he was going to have descendants who would do incredible things, and their kids would do incredible things, and so on and so on until his descendants would be as countless as the stars.

When Abraham first heard this speech from God, he was pumped! He was like, "Let's do this thing." He waited with eager anticipation. *Will it be tomorrow? The next day? The next?!* He stood by, waiting for these amazing promised kiddos, waiting to become the father of nations.

He stayed up at night, dreaming about songs kids thousands and thousands of years later would sing in their Sunday school classes about him.

"Father Abraham had many sons. Many sons had Father Abraham. Right arm! Left arm! Turn around! Sit down."

He even came up with a dance. Needless to say, he was getting carried away with hope.

Then a year went by.

And another.

And another.

"Uh . . . God? Are you there?" Abraham said. "You're still gonna do this whole countless-stars descendants thing, right? I mean, I already wrote the song, went out and bought hundreds of diapers and onesies, told the entire neighborhood about it. I mean, we're still cool, right?"

Suddenly Abraham's wife was past her childbearing years. The twenties came and left. The thirties flew right by. When she approached her fififties, Abraham's hope should have been shattered. I mean, they were entering impossible territory! Sarah couldn't physically have a child. How was this going to work?

When Paul, who lived thousands of years after Abraham, talked about this season of Abraham's life, he said, "Against all hope, Abraham in hope believed and so became the father of many nations" (Rom. 4:18). Abraham had hope against hope, meaning he believed in God's promises when it no longer made any sense.

One night Abraham was kicking it with God in the tent, and God finally got a little bit more specific about his promises. "Sarah is going to get pregnant," God said.

"Uh . . . what?" It was one of those record-scratch, spit-take moments. "You do know she's like ninety years old and has hip problems, right? We talking about the same Sarah?" Abraham heard a huge laugh coming from the tent next door.

"Ha!"

It was Sarah. She overheard what God had said, and now she was in a fit of laughter. "Me?" she managed to say between laughs. "Having a little baby? Bahahaha." She was LOL-ing all over the tent.

The thought of it seemed crazy, lunatic, against common sense. But that's the audacity of hope. And sure enough, nine months later, their son was born, just as God had promised. They named him Isaac, which in Hebrew basically means "ROFL"—because God doing something that impossible is pretty laughable when you think about it.

HOPE DEFERRED

It's easy when things aren't going exactly how we imagined to lose hope or joy for the future. Remember Proverbs 13:12? It says, "Hope deferred makes the heart sick, but a longing fulfilled is a tree of life."

We've all experienced that ache when something we've hoped for doesn't quite work out. Since Julia and I imagined our daughter being healthy and growing into a volleyball player while she was still in the womb, we obviously experienced a feeling of sickness when it didn't seem that was possible. All parents hope for amazing things for their children, and when they're forced to encounter the exact opposite, they are brokenhearted.

For me this heartsickness often occurs during life's giant transitions. Many times in my life I've moved away from cities to pursue a new door that's been opened. For some reason, each time I leave a city behind, I feel as though a dream has been dashed.

"Dang. I could've done more. I could've been more to the people there. If I had only had one more year."

I spent nine years pastoring in Puyallup, Washington. I watched our youth ministry and young adult ministry grow. I formed close friendships and watched many lives change. But I had so many more dreams of what the group could be and of who else in the city we could reach. Despite these dreams, Julia and I both felt it was time to go somewhere else.

Even though I was excited about the next adventure waiting for us in Seattle, I felt as though I was leaving something undone in Puyallup. Everything I had poured my life into, my work, what we had established, I was now leaving behind.

Transition, for me, has always been a marker of heartsickness and hope deferred. As I drove away from Oak Harbor, when I left LA, and when we packed up in Puyallup, I left feeling a little sick, wishing I could've had more time.

HOPE FULFILLED

The beauty of Proverbs 13:12 is that it doesn't deny the very human, painful reaction we have when hope seems lost, but it illustrates how it feels when things do work out for the good.

"A longing fulfilled is a tree of life."

Three years before writing this book, we felt God speaking to us to start a church in Los Angeles. I had always loved LA, where I went to school and first began youth pastoring, and God was calling me back there. Julia and I talked about it, prayed about it, and got excited about what lay ahead for us.

And then came April 10, 2012. When we heard Georgia's diagnosis, everything was put on pause. Talk about hope deferred.

God, you put this dream in my heart, and now I don't get to go do it? What was the point of that? I felt an awful lot like Abraham, wondering how this whole promise thing was going to play out.

Our life was completely changed after April 10. No longer was it "Where are we going to go? What are we going to do next?" Our conversations changed to: "How can we take more time to rest? Where can I cut back on preaching every week? How can we focus on our family instead of leading for a season?"

It was hard on our identity as a family. Life was not going how we had planned. A few springs after living in Seattle and serving at a church while resting with my family, I felt God remind me of this dream again. It felt like the right time to do what I had been called to do.

California, here we come.

Julia and I began planning, dreaming, getting everything in order; and months later, we were driving, two babies packed in car seats, all our stuff shoved into a trailer, to a new home waiting for us in Los Angeles.

Like the proverb says, I felt alive. I was exuberant, ecstatic, smiling from ear to ear! I mean, I was walking around searching for anyone, strangers even, to give me a fist pound. I needed 24–7 fist pounds! That's how good I felt.

Today, we now lead Zoe Church LA. *Zoe* in Greek means "abundant life," because that's what this new season is to us—a "longing fulfilled," a "tree of life." Every meeting, every gathering we have as we build this amazing group of people—they have been on my heart for years. And here it is, coming to pass.

Hope fulfilled.

WHERE DO YOU PUT YOUR HOPE?

How tragic would it be to believe that there's a God who created the universe, to believe in the stories, songs, poems, and letters of the Bible, to believe in Jesus and in the Holy Spirit, and to have all the faith in the world, but to not have any hope?

I have hope that something better is around the corner for Julia and me. I have hope that God will give Georgia a safe arrival, that whether in this life or the next, my daughter will be able to live to the fullest. She will be able to run, to talk, to dance, and more. Hope is carrying me through today's aspirating woes and seizures. Hope is carrying Julia and me through life with a handicapped daughter who cannot communicate her needs to us.

As you face life's trials and storms, what is it that you're hoping for? I know that it's easy to feel like giving up and it may seem embarrassing to have an audacious kind of hope that works against common sense, but it's time to grab onto something that can carry you through tomorrow.

Perhaps it's not so difficult for you to list out what you hope for. Perhaps it's more difficult for you to answer the question, "Who do you place your hope in?" Maybe people have failed you time and again (which people tend to do). Maybe your dreams have been dashed or you've experienced failed expectations and life is not going how you planned. It's time to place your hope in Jesus.

Psalm 33:17–19 says, "A horse is a vain hope for deliverance; despite all its great strength it cannot save. But the eyes of the LORD are on those who fear him, on those whose hope is in his unfailing love, to deliver them from death and keep them alive in famine."

I know you probably don't own a horse or relate to the first portion of this psalm. But replace *horse* with *doctor, medicine, drugs, romance, my own strength,* or *fame,* and you may begin to realize what David is talking about. Often if we do have any hope at all, we're hoping in all the wrong things.

I know for Georgia, time and time again, Julia and I have placed hope in medicine or a doctor's words and seen only failure. But as I look back on our journey so far and remember the moments when we've been able to face the next day, when we've felt the burden lifted or felt great joy, I realize these were the moments when we had placed our hope in God.

He will keep you alive when common sense says you should be

dead. He will bless you when the world says you should be poor and alone. He will deliver you when you're experiencing pain and suffering. He will give you more and more. This is what I'm eagerly anticipating. This is where I put my hope.

Chapter Ten

IT JUST GETS BETTER

AND BETTER

I'D HAVE A HARD TIME FINDING A PERSON WHO LIKES IT WHEN things get worse as the days go by. "Oh yeah . . . me? I love eating rotten food. I'm stoked when my car breaks down! And when the stock I bought shares in yesterday suddenly crashes? Oh, that's my favorite!"

People who say these things do not exist. This is because we aren't happy when things go from good to bad or from bad to worse. We want our situation to improve day by day.

We like it when things get better.

Personally, I find that a lot of things around me are getting better. Technology, for instance. I'm thankful that technology only gets better with time. A new social media, a faster computer, a more advanced camera on the iPhone—we're all thankful for these things. Technology continues to improve year after year. The battery life, on the other hand . . . Well, let's just say the struggle is real when it comes to the battery life. I will never understand how the geniuses of our time can create these amazing devices that allow all the information of the world to fit in our small pockets, but they can't solve our battery-life problems. Figure it out already, Tim Cook.

Food also gets better. And prettier. French toast for breakfast?

Put a filter on it. Thanksgiving turkey dinner? Put a filter on it, add some pretty text overlay, and Instagram that cranberry sauce.

You used to be able to grab a Big Mac and eat it alone in the car. Now everything we eat must be posted for all to see. That means that the Big Mac is being replaced by green smoothies, kale salads, and other things that taste better, look prettier, and make us feel better.

Even church gets better with time. I, for one, am very thankful for this.

If you grew up being forced to go to church, you know this is true. It used to be that tambourines and people twirling flags were synonymous with church—especially if that church happened to be charismatic in nature. Unfortunately, I had personal experiences with both as a youth. Growing up as a pastor's kid in a charismatic circle, I have indeed encountered the good, the bad, and the ugly when it comes to church.

This is the church.
This is the steeple.
Open it up and see all the people . . .
. . . who are crazy.

As a kid in a small, 1990s church, my job was to run the overhead projector. For all you children, an overhead projector is a device that shines a light on a table and reflects the image onto a wall. To show lyrics for all the church to see, someone would have to physically man this device. Meaning, as the song transitions, someone would have to move one sheet of plastic with words on it and place a new sheet of plastic with words on it onto the table. And that someone was me.

As the congregation sang their twentieth round of "Shout to the Lord," my dad would slap me on the back of the head if I wasn't quick enough to get the right lyrics onto the projector in time for the congregation to sing them.

The back of my head and I are happy that church is better today. I know somewhere in middle America someone is still waving a flag and banging a tambourine down the aisle, and bless your heart, Sister Susie. But many churches today have amazing buildings, fresh designs, excellent music, great lighting, and, ladies and gentlemen, the miracle of PowerPoint.

We like it when things get better.

I've found one thing to be certain as I've journeyed through life and experienced my ups and my downs: life with Jesus just gets better and better. So to anyone who is a fan of better, I'd have to strongly urge you to try this life out for yourself. And if you think you're already living it and everything seems to be getting worse, you might be doing something wrong.

First Corinthians 2:9 (NLT) puts it this way: "No mind has imagined what God has prepared for those who love him."

When I read something like that, I realize this is only the beginning.

Gone Fishing

There's a story in Luke 5 where a man named Simon Peter learns a certain lesson about this concept of "better."

What you need to know about Simon Peter, besides the fact that he has two first names, is that he was a fisherman. And fishermen back in the day in Galilee liked to fish in the middle of the night. These were the OGs of the fishing world. Because the daytime is terribly hot in the Middle East, nighttime was the way to go for Simon and his buddies.

It was morning after a long night of fishing in Galilee, and Simon Peter and his team were bringing in their two fishing boats.

Empty. These men, whose *profession* was fishing, had come home empty-handed. They had caught zero fish. That's like a baker going to work and staring at some flour all day before coming home without baking a single loaf of bread. All in all, the situation was downright embarrassing.

As they packed up for the day, Simon Peter tried halfheartedly to encourage his team. He tried not to be seen, thinking he could never live down the shame of returning home with empty boats and no fish.

"Yeah, uh, we'll get 'em tomorrow, guys!" he told his team, completely feigning optimism.

And then he saw his worst nightmare. A huge crowd of people quickly approaching the scene of his terrible embarrassment.

Let me tell you about this crowd. Jesus was leading it, and Jesus could draw a *lot* of people. It seemed this guy from Nazareth couldn't go anywhere without a huge group of people following him, waiting for his next tweetable moment or his next miraculous act. But Jesus had a heart for these crowds. He didn't try to push them away or roll his eyes as they asked for more. Instead, he tried to find creative ways to communicate to all of them at once.

There Jesus was, swarmed by tons of people whom he loved, and he had no platform or pulpit to speak from. How were they all going to hear him?

This is where Jesus got creative. As he looked around, wondering how he was going to preach to the multitudes, he got what might be the first ever Pinterest-worthy idea. He saw Simon Peter trying to bring his boat in after a long night of work and realized the boat might do the trick. Bam. DIY platform by Jesus.

Excited about this problem-solving revelation, Jesus hurried over to Simon and asked if he could borrow his boat. Simon agreed. "It's not doing me any good."

And Jesus got on the boat and preached.

And the crowd went wild.

In that moment, Jesus was able to teach the crowd and meet their needs. But when he was done preaching and the crowd left, Jesus turned to the depressed fisherman whose boat he'd borrowed.

"Simon, why don't you and I go out into the deep?" he said. "Let's just get away for a sec."

This is God. He has an amazing ability to meet the needs of the crowd, yet he still wants personal time with us. He's always concerned about the one. And in that moment Simon was the one.

After they rowed the boat out away from the shore, Jesus turned to Simon and said, "Simon. Indulge me. Why don't you drop that net of yours over the boat and see if we catch anything?"

This was what Simon was afraid of. He stared at the water for a moment, then up at the sky. "Oh, is that a bird . . . over there . . . I swear I saw one." He was trying to do something, anything, to distract from his total failure. Finally, he looked at Jesus.

"Uh . . . I don't know how to tell you this, but we fished all night last night. All night. And we didn't catch *anything.*"

Here Simon was, confessing to Jesus that he had failed at his job. He told him that despite his best efforts he'd fallen short. "I tried, but I failed," he finally said, sincerely.

And Jesus simply replied, "Nah. It's fine. Just throw your net over for a catch!"

"Last night was a bust, and we never fish during the day," Simon said. "This is unorthodox. In fact, this is just plain weird!"

Then he paused a moment. Jesus seemed so sure.

"But nevertheless, at your word, I will obey," Simon finally said.

And just like that, he threw the net over. What happened next is what always seems to happen with God. The net began to break because it was so full of fish.

Simon started freaking out and calling for help. Two men would not be able to handle the hundreds of fish that were filling his net! In the distance, he spotted his guys, finishing up their packing for the day. Their nets were washed and their boats tied up.

"Help!" he yelled out to his compadres. "Get your boats out here. Now!"

The boat was so full of fish it started to sink. Simon was shocked by the whole event. He went from two empty boats to two boats sinking from the weight of the fish that filled them.

Things got way better for Simon Peter.

And with all this better, all this overflowing fishy goodness, how did Simon respond? Did he start strutting around like, "What? Yeah, me? Yeah, I fished this. I can fish all night and day! Because that's how amazing I am"?

Did he start walking around with entitlement, telling others the formula for success?

Did he brag about all the stuff he did to get blessed by Jesus—the Bible he read, the bumper sticker he bought, how many times he prayed, attended church, practiced religion, etc.?

No. Instead of falling into that empty, void, meaningless mindset, Simon fell straight to his knees.

"God! Stop. This is too much! It's way too much!" Simon said when they got to the shore, boats filled to the brim with fish.

"For a sinner like me, this is too much goodness. You know where I've lived; you know what I've done. I don't deserve this. I never dreamed this. This wasn't a part of my ten-year goals for my life. It's . . . it's too much."

Jesus had given Simon better than he deserved.

It Doesn't Always Make Sense

Simon Peter did something that made little sense. He fished in the daytime. He threw his net out when he knew the water had run dry and given him nothing during his entire night's work. And yet, he still did it. He said to Jesus, "Nevertheless!" and tossed his net over.

This is not an easy feat to accomplish. Today, answers are so close to our fingertips and only a Google search away. We long to understand something before we pursue it. We read the how-tos, the instruction manuals; we listen to the podcasts. We want to be prepared and fully grasp where we're heading next. It's not normal, in this day and age, for someone to just do something without understanding it first. And yet, the Bible says, "Trust in the LORD with all your heart, and lean not on your own understanding" (Prov. 3:5 NKJV).

Have you ever been asked to do something that simply does not make sense? I remember in high school having a friend whose mother had values similar to my mother's. Both of our crazy moms would wake us up early on Saturday mornings to do chores.

Yes, I grew up loathing Saturday mornings. And my friend did too. One day, while exchanging notes on the new tortures our moms had tried out the previous Saturday, my friend told me, "I had the worst chore day in the history of chore days."

He proceeded to describe a terrible Saturday. At 7:30 in the morning, his mom woke him up and said, "Get out of bed. We're gonna wash the car."

I grew up in the Pacific Northwest, where it rains 97 percent of the time. And that Saturday was no different.

My friend looked out the window and said, "Mom, it's raining. Raining!"

"You don't think I know that?" she replied. "Get your butt out of bed! We're gonna wash the car."

So my friend had to stand outside in the pouring rain, washing the car.

"When I was done washing, Chad, is when it got real bad. I

started walking into my house, thinking I was done, right? And then my mom walks out and throws me a towel and says, 'Dry it off!'"

Uh . . . what?

Drying off a car in the pouring rain makes about as much sense as throwing a net into a sea with no fish. But that's what God does. He sometimes asks us to do things that make little sense. He urges us, tugs us, pulls us away to get out of our natural mind-set. He tells us things such as, "Believe that your handicapped daughter is going to get healed, and tell the world about it."

I don't know about you, but I want to respond the way Peter did. When God asks Julia and me to step out and believe things for Georgia, I want to respond with: "Nevertheless, at your word, I will obey." I want to respond this way because I want something better!

OVERFLOW

It's important to note that Jesus didn't return things to their original state for Peter. Instead, he gave him more than enough. He gave him too much! He didn't simply give him one day's worth of fish, but instead caused two boats to be filled.

We are not talking about a stingy God. We see time and time again through the Bible a God who doesn't only give exactly what someone needs. He gives more. At the end of the story in Luke 9, when Jesus multiplied the fishes and loaves for the hungry crowd, it says, "They all ate and were satisfied, and the disciples picked up twelve basketfuls of broken pieces that were left over" (v. 17). Jesus satisfies, he meets our needs, he feeds us when we're hungry, he provides a day's work when we need it. But he doesn't stop there. We're talking about a God who goes above and beyond.

Even in his very first miracle, Jesus proved this. When his mother asked him to help with a wedding celebration, Jesus didn't turn one barrel of water into some decent, standard wine and call it good. He filled six jars, and each of these jars could hold up to thirty gallons. That's 180 gallons of wine! But he didn't stop there. He filled them with the most delicious wine. In John 2:10, the master of the wedding banquet says, "Everyone brings out the choice wine first and then the cheaper wine after the guests have had too much to drink; but you have saved the best till now." He not only met the needs of the wedding; he also gave them a better celebration than any of the wedding guests could have imagined.

I think that when we ask God for something, we often think too small. We ask for what we need and nothing more.

"God, provide a job for me so I can provide for my family," instead of, "God, provide my dream job for me, one where I'm thriving, one where I can see wealth grow and have enough money to be hugely generous and bless other people." We need to read these stories about Jesus and realize that this is the God we're working with. He's ready to overflow our boat and give us more than we need.

This overflowing nature of God is also seen in the story of Job. I've mentioned Job previously. Job is always mentioned when individuals are coping with terrible loss and horrible circumstances, because we can say, "Hey, at least we're not Job."

Job lost his kids. He lost his riches. And on top of all this, he had boils all over his body. But after this happened, after he walked through the storm and the dust and the ashes, the story ends with a bang. And by bang, I mean epilogue. In the epilogue of Job's story, God restored to him twice as much as he had before. He had more than he started with!

I don't know why we're always expecting some sort of punishment from God. We fail at some moment in life, we lose a job, we yell at our spouse, we ruin a relationship, we gossip, we lie, we cheat, and we go to him with our heads hanging low expecting him to ground us or disown us. What we're forgetting in these moments is that we're going to our Father.

Sometimes I imagine what it would be like to have a day or a moment with Georgia when she can laugh, walk, and talk like a three-year-old. I imagine getting this glimpse, maybe merely twenty-four hours, when I can see how God intended her to be.

I imagine her talking to me, playing with me, running around, being a kid. Let's say I do get to this moment with her, and all of a sudden, Georgia does something wrong. She throws a fit or disobeys. She screams or yells or doesn't want to give me a hug.

How do you think I would respond?

I've waited three years to have a relationship with my little girl. I've been desperate for a chance to talk to her. Do you think I'd take it out on her or disown her if she started disobeying in that moment?

If Georgia came up to me and asked me for something, I would give her *anything* she asked for. On top of that, I would search for a way to give her more. Too many toys, too many hugs, too much ice cream . . . I would find a way to bless my little girl.

This is how God feels about us.

Matthew 7:11 says, "If you, then, though you are evil, know how to give good gifts to your children, how much more will your Father in heaven give good gifts to those who ask him!"

God is a perfect Father who wants to give us more than we could ever want or ask for. He loves us even more than I love my own kids, because he doesn't make any mistakes. He thinks of time away with you the way I think of this kind of moment with my daughter, Georgia.

"If only I could talk with them. If only I could relate with them. If only I could be with them."

He loves you, and he wants to give you more than you started with. This is why he had Peter row the boat out deeper into the water. He wanted time with Peter just as he wants time with you and me. He doesn't want our lives to stay in the shallow end, where there's envy, lust, greed, and emptiness. He wants us to experience deepness with him, where he can bless us with more than we've ever had before.

WAX ON

"First, wash all car. Then wax. Wax on . . . Wax off."

Sometimes, I like to imagine Jesus as Mr. Miyagi from *The Karate Kid*.

All that little Daniel wanted to do was learn karate and be the best. So he goes to Mr. Miyagi, karate guru extraordinaire, for lessons. And what does Mr. Miyagi do?

He takes him to the backyard and has him paint the fence. Then he has him wash the car. All he wanted to do was learn karate! And here's Daniel, in the backyard, painting a fence. *What in the world? This ain't no karate!*

You might be in a position where you're asking, "God, why?"

You're wondering why he's placed some obstacle in your life, some situation that's keeping you from achieving a dream, succeeding in your profession, or from being healthy or happy.

"God, why? Why are you having me paint the fence, wash the car in the rain, or take my boat out when I know I'm a failure?"

You just wait. Something's coming.

I don't want to spoil the ending of a cinematic masterpiece, but Daniel eventually learns karate. And he doesn't just learn karate; he succeeds and wins! Somehow those obscure lessons lead him to a place where everything gets better.

"God, why? Why am I here? This doesn't make any sense." This might be what your prayers sound like. I know that in our situation with Georgia, I have prayed this time and time again. "Why, God? What's the point of all this? Can we be done now, please? Thank you."

But God is one step ahead. He's leading, he's planning, and he's providing.

At the end of the overflowing fish moment with Simon, after he fell to his knees saying he didn't deserve any of this, Jesus looked at him and asked him to get up.

"Come on, get up, Simon! Get up. I gotta tell you a little something. You know, I'm changing this whole thing up. I'm changing your whole purpose."

In this moment, Jesus changed Simon Peter's life.

"From now on, I'm going to make you a fisher of men. Your life is going to be about people. I'm changing your destiny."

And just like that, the men pulled their boats ashore, dropped their nets, and left everything. They followed Jesus. And God had a lot better in store for them.

God may take you through unique situations or ask you to risk it all and try something ridiculous, but why? Why does he do this? It's all because he wants us to follow him. Because a life with him is better than a life on our own. It's better than our best day at work and better than any bank account we could ever accomplish.

These things seem absolutely meaningless when compared to following.

Obviously, my story shows that just because you follow him doesn't mean your life will be without storms. You won't be exempt from pain, sorrow, or smooth brain. Simon Peter didn't go on to live a perfect life without making mistakes or experiencing pain. No, he had to watch some of his best friends get killed and tortured, including Jesus!

No, pain is real, and because we live in this world, there's no formula for avoiding it. But there is a safe arrival at the end of this journey if you follow Jesus. Not only that, but he will strengthen you along the way.

When you're facing something with Jesus by your side, you'll discover a life beyond your wildest dreams. And the best part? It only gets better and better.

In Conclusion . . .

Are you ready to celebrate what is to come? We've established that pain is a reality. We aren't promised a life free of harm, and though some may experience worse storms and tragedies than others, we will all encounter a terrible season in our lifetime.

We've also established that God is a reality. He's there when we need him most, he's capable of healing any illness and rescuing you from any dark place, he's strong, he's faithful, and he loves you no matter what.

We've discussed what to do with this information. How do we respond to such a big God with such unconditional love? When our daughter is having her thousandth seizure or throwing up her hundredth meal, we cannot lie to ourselves and believe that we did something to deserve this. We must turn our eyes toward the healer and comforter and rest in the fact that he loves us no matter what and will lead us out of this situation.

Now that we know all this, we must believe that he has good things in store for us in this life. As Ephesians 3:20 states, what comes next is something beyond "your wildest dreams" (THE MESSAGE). Throughout the Bible and the stories we've discussed, we see God restoring exceedingly above what people such as Ruth, Job, and Peter had before they started. My hope is that these stories, along with my story, reveal God's plan to prosper you even in the midst of your calamity.

It would be heartbreaking to me if you simply read this story about a little girl who doctors say doesn't have much of a chance for a normal life and simply shed a tear, close the book, and walk away. If you leave saying "that's nice" or "poor Chad," I will have failed you.

My aim is to reveal to you that despite trials there is a real God who can offer hope for the future. As my wife and I have learned to hope even while facing a terrible situation, my prayer is that you, too, learn to hope "against hope" like Abraham. That when you look at your situation and feel it's too impossible or huge to overcome, you find the God who gives you hope beyond human rationality.

Action Steps

My prayer is that you do something next, that you believe in the better, and that you leave this book filled with anticipation, knowing God has the very best in store for you! If you need a place to start, here are eight statements I've found to be true and to work when I've been forced to face Georgia's disorder and all that comes with it. They've lifted my burden and made smiling at the future possible. I hope they will do the same for you.

1. Don't stop at faith. Have hope!

"And now these three remain: faith, *hope* and love" (1 Cor. 13:13, emphasis added).

Faith is having complete trust and confidence in God. It is vital to Christianity. We must trust that God is real, that Jesus is his Son, and that he sent his Son to die for us and forgive us of our sins.

I've found that many Christians make faith a priority, but hope is not inferior to faith. It's important to believe in the unseen, but it's just as important to expect and anticipate that something better is coming next. We can believe that Jesus is real, but we can't stop there. We need to have hope that he will positively change us, that we will live in eternity with him, and that we'll see him do amazing things in our lifetimes.

We need to hope, not only with an optimistic outlook or wishful thinking without proof, but with confident expectation based on solid certainty.

2. Don't put your hope in people or situations; put your hope in God.

Psalm 20:7 says, "Some trust in chariots and some in horses, but we trust in the name of the LORD our God."

Where do you place your trust? Placement is power. You can't go around throwing your hope all over town, trusting in things that are fleeting. I think it's easy to place our hope in people and expect they'll come through for us when we need them most or step up in the day of trouble. But remember that like you, people are human. Think of all the times you've failed someone or when certain limitations on your time or money have prevented you from helping friends the way they needed. Humans are full of restrictions. This doesn't mean you can't trust your friends or family to help; it means you should not place unhealthy hope in them. They cannot be everything that you need them to be.

Similarly, situations are constantly changing. You might think a job promotion is coming or that you'll be able to save up to buy a house, and then your circumstances change. This is why we can't place our hope in these ever-changing things. We need to place our hope in God. Hebrews 13:8 says, "Jesus Christ is the same yesterday and today and forever." He is a constant, and because of this, we can expect him to heal, to restore, to bring peace, and ultimately, to rescue us from our situations.

3. The darker the night, the greater the sunrise.

"Weeping may stay for the night, but rejoicing comes in the morning" (Ps. 30:5).

Imagine sitting in a dark room. You can't make out shapes or colors. All is black. Suddenly someone turns on the light, and the entire room rushes with color. It's brighter than you remembered it before the lights went off because of the pitch-black darkness you were sitting in moments earlier. This is what happens when we come out of our dark circumstances. Often, the worse our situation is, the greater the light at the end of the tunnel.

I believe that God leaves us better than we started. Things might be terrible for you right now. You may be facing the worst possible situation. But the Bible says, "Rejoicing comes in the morning."

4. This is just a minor setback for a major comeback.

Remember that God can restore things back to their original state and then some! This means that you may not only get your healing; you may also find that life is fuller and more blessed than it was before you got sick. Sometimes our miracle doesn't happen the way we imagined it would. For instance, I would have liked to have seen Georgia healed instantly at the moment of Diagnosis Day when the first tweets went out. God often has a different plan. But we need to realize that this plan is above and beyond what we could conceive ourselves.

There is a major comeback for you. Don't view your situation as impossible; view it the way God views it—a minor bump in the road that you will overcome!

5. The best is yet to come!

It isn't bad to remember or reflect on the past, but to view history as the "glory days" or the "best days" can be dangerous. Looking at life this way can prevent you from anticipating all the great things that God has placed in front of you.

Your best days are not behind you, distant memories for you to talk about. They're in front of you, waiting! As Christians, we need to stop this disease of nostalgia. We must look forward to the great adventure that is life with God.

6. The big time is where you are.

It's important to have a positive perspective about where you currently are. Yes, look to the future with expectation. Yes, remember the things God has done for you in the past and let it build your faith. But also, learn to be content with where you are right now at this very moment. Understand that this is exactly where God has placed you.

Don't wait until tomorrow to praise him or turn to him. This is your moment. This is your big time to shine and start walking in the promises he has for you. As much as you need hope for the future, you also need hope for today.

7. Love life!

This is one of my favorite personal mantras. I love confusing people with my story. I love seeing the looks on their faces when they hear about my daughter's illness and see how I still truly love life and take pleasure in living it to its fullest amidst all the heartache of my situation. This is the best way to get back at the enemy. Sitting in sorrow and pain is exactly what the devil wants, but you can find a way to appreciate life even in the darkest of times.

Life, God, and people are to be enjoyed. So get out there and enjoy them!

8. Remember: "this too shall pass."

"He has made everything beautiful in its time" (Eccl. 3:11).

When you're in the middle of something truly terrible, your thoughts can turn dark quickly. They can spiral out of control if you let them, telling you that you will never get out of this or you won't survive.

I am here to tell you that you will. You're going to make it out of your circumstance, and you will see the other side. In "its time," your situation will become beautiful. When you get to that side, you'll be able to look back on these events and thank God for bringing you through.

Where Are We Now?

As for the Veaches, we still reside in sunny Los Angeles, where we pastor ZOE LA. Though the pain of our circumstances hasn't yet passed, God has truly blessed our family. Our lil gangsta Dub-C continues to grow and get wilder every day, and we're about to begin a new adventure with a third baby (Lord, help us all).

This life of ours is full, and our house is literally getting fuller each day. Georgia may not be healed and this disorder may still be our reality, but we've seen her do better than the doctors ever anticipated. She still struggles with seizures, aspiration, and muscle control, but despite these, she finds ways to communicate with us by kicking and making noises.

Every day Julia and I strive to give her the best life we can. We're grateful for her health and how far she's come, but we continue to do more tests and seek more answers. We never stop clinging to hope, despite how impossible it may seem to doctors or the world around us.

When we chose Georgia's name before she was born, people would respond with their best, soulful Ray Charles impression and sing out "Georgia on My Mind." Surprisingly, this little lyric has been true not only for me, but for so many around the world. Our girl has been on people's hearts and minds. Many have prayed every day that God would heal her and give our family that safe arrival.

For me, it's not simply a prayer, a want, an ask, or a need. It's not merely something I have to say because I am a pastor and so often find myself on a platform before many attentive ears. I truly believe in the unreasonable.

I have seen darker days come and go. I have learned from God through them all and seen his amazing ability to come alongside, to love, to comfort, and to rescue my family. It would take me months to list every example of love and support we've received from the community around us. God has gone above and beyond.

Because I have seen all this, I know that tomorrow will be better. I have hope against hope that Georgia's brain will not be smooth for eternity, that she will walk and talk, if not in this life, then in the next. I have hope that our family, even this newest member about to enter the world, will come out of this stronger than when we started.

As we walk out this life, we'll continue to put our faith in the who behind it all, the one who is faithful in suffering, the only true remedy, who takes the pain and makes it into something more, something better, something beautiful.

ACKNOWLEDGMENTS

Jesus, julia, our kids, zoe church, and our team.
leslie, esther, roman, and the thomas nelson crew.
our parents.
our pastors, judah and chelsea smith.
all of our friends who have stood with us through the fire . . .
we love you and are forever grateful.
the best is yet to come.

NOTES

CHAPTER THREE: DAUGHTER NAMED RUTH

1. "Dave Chappelle & Maya Angelou," *Iconoclasts*, season 2, episode 6, directed by Joe Berlinger, aired November 30, 2006.
2. Martin Luther King, Jr., *The Papers of Martin Luther King, Jr.: Volume VI: The Advocate of the Social Gospel: September 1948–March 1963*, ed. Clayborne Carson (Berkeley: University of California Press, 2007), 344.

PART 2: SOMEBODY FEED GEORGIA

1. "NINDS Lissencephaly Information Page," National Institute of Neurological Disorders and Stroke, last modified April 16, 2014, http://www.ninds.nih.gov/disorders/lissencephaly/lissencephaly.htm.

CHAPTER SEVEN: THE LANGUAGE OF LOVE

1. Gary D. Chapman, *The Five Love Languages: How to Express Heartfelt Commitment to Your Mate* (Chicago: Northfield, 2004).

CHAPTER NINE: WHO MOVED MY HOPE?

1. G. K. Chesterton, *Heretics* (Rockville, MD: Serenity Publishers, 2009), 82.

ABOUT THE AUTHOR

CHAD VEACH IS THE PASTOR OF ZOE CHURCH IN LOS ANGELES, California. Chad and his wife, Julia, have three beautiful children, Georgia Estelle, Winston Charles, and Maverick Montgomery. Chad travels stateside and internationally bringing a message of hope.

Twitter: www.twitter.com/chadcveach
Instagram: www.instagram.com/chad_veach
Facebook: www.facebook.com/chadcveach
www.zoechurch.org